DESTRUCTIVE GOAL PURSUIT

DESTRUCTIVE GOAL PURSUIT

The Mount Everest Disaster

D. Christopher Kayes, PhD

First published 2006 by
PALGRAVE MACMILLAN
Houndmills, Basingstoke, Hampshire RG21 6XS and
175 Fifth Avenue, New York, N.Y. 10010
Companies and representatives throughout the world

PALGRAVE MACMILLAN is the global academic imprint of the Palgrave
Macmillan division of St. Martin's Press, LLC and of Palgrave Macmillan Ltd.
Macmillan® is a registered trademark in the United States, United Kingdom
and other countries. Palgrave is a registered trademark in the European
Union and other countries.

ISBN-13: 978–0–230–00332–3
ISBN-10: 0–230–00332–X

This book is printed on paper suitable for recycling and made form fully
managed and sustained forest sources.

A catalogue record for this book is available from the British Library.

Library of Congress Cataloging-in-Publication Data
Kayes, D. Christopher.
   Destructive goal pursuit : the Mt. Everest disaster / by D. Christopher Kayes.
      p.   cm.
   Includes bibliographical references and index.
   Contents: Learning from the Everest disaster—Destructive goal pursuit—
   From destructive to productive pursuit—Rethinking leadership in
   organizations.
   ISBN 0–230–00332–X
   1. Goal setting in personnel management.   2. Leadership.   3. Teams in
   the workplace.   4. Mountaineering accidents—Everest, Mount (China and
   Nepal)   I. Title.
   HF5549.5.G6K39 2006
   658.4'092—dc22   2006045367

10   9   8   7   6   5   4   3   2   1
15   14   13   12   11   10   09   08   07   06

Printed and bound in Great Britain by
Creative Print & Design (Wales), Ebbw Vale

Dedication

To Anna, Braden, and Ben, may you have the passion to seek great heights and the wisdom to turn around, and to Rob Hall and Scott Fischer, whose experience taught me more about leadership than textbooks.

Contents

Foreword

By identifying the negative and potentially disastrous consequences of the non reflective pursuit of ambitious goals, this book offers a sage warning to those of us who live in a culture where high goals are a praiseworthy status symbol and relentless pursuit of them a sign of moral superiority. Leaders who set high goals and pursue them regardless of the consequences are seen as principled, while the leader who learns from experience and modifies goals accordingly runs the risk of being seen as "wishy-washy." Children are encouraged from an early age to "dream the impossible dream" and to strive toward the highest goals. Writing this foreword from our winter home in laid-back Molokai, Hawaii, we are reminded of a popular saying here—"Goals are deceptive: The un-aimed arrow never misses."

Nearly 10 years prior to the publication of this book, Professor Kayes, then a doctoral student, presented a paper as part of his coursework. The paper described how a group of mountain climbers lost their way and how their failure to learn in the face of change lead to their eventual death. Over the course of the next few years, Professor Kayes refined his thinking, reviewed what seemed to be hundreds of research documents, and then vigorously wrote and rewrote drafts of the original paper. All of this is to say that the book you are about to read represents the culmination of a lot of work and thoughtfully directed attention. This book is, itself, a positive example of its main message: illustrating a process of goal achievement motivated by an intrinsic desire to learn.

We have not spent much time climbing mountains so making the leap from mountain climbing to management was not easy for us. Yet, something in the story resonated with our experience. It was not until years later that we began to understand the implications of the mountain climbing accident for our own experience. Like most of us that live in the contemporary world, we have experienced both the benefits and the downsides of ambitious pursuit of goals. The mountain climbing accident recounted in this book provides a vivid example of what can happen when people focus on accomplishing narrow goals at the expense of learning.

Unlike many of the growing number of books that reveal lessons from adventure and tragedy, this book is more complex. The lessons are not simple and the advice given for leaders is not easy to digest. This book does not lay out a simple step-by-step framework for what it takes to be a good leader. But Professor Kayes's central message seems not to be a complicated one. Learning to be a leader takes time, patience, and a serious look into one's own motives, abilities, and experience.

This book makes an important contribution to the experiential learning perspective on leadership, showing how knowledge and learning are core attributes of the successful leader. If, as some have suggested, learning is the only competitive advantage, then leaders need first and foremost to be learners. Leadership is not simply about being charismatic or influential or visionary. Leadership requires developing others to help deal with challenging situations on their own. As Professor Kayes says, "The primary role of the leader is not to direct attention of others toward goals, but rather toward learning" (p. 203). The book provides a warning to those who fail to see learning as a primary factor in successful leadership. As Kayes shows, goals are important for motivating and developing; however, when narrow goals force learning to take a backseat in the minds of leaders, they are courting disaster.

Professor Kayes analysis of the Everest disaster deepens the interpretation of its tragic implications by drawing on classic thinkers on leadership and learning such as Kurt Lewin, Abraham Maslow, and W.F. Bion as well as others influential in the field of organizational behavior. By showing how these thinkers remain relevant today, Professor Kayes continues a tradition of experiential learning that focuses on how theory can help solve real world problems.

As an example of systematic research, Professor Kayes's study represents two emerging trends in the study of experiential learning. First, there is growing interest in looking more closely at the qualitative side of learning from experience. Using a variety of qualitative methods including thematic analysis, narrative, and conversational analysis, researchers are beginning to describe the richness of how individuals use experience as the basis for learning. Based as it is on an award-winning journal article, this work offers an outstanding example of how qualitative methods can be used to develop and test theory and generate implications for practice. The rich description of how the climbers learned from, or in many cases failed to learn from, their own experience shows that relevance of the learning cycle for teams and organizations. Second, there is growing interest is how individual learning relates to teams. In recent years, a number of systematic studies have examined how individual experience is transformed into team learning. This research clarifies thinking on how learning is carried forward in teams and through conversation.

We feel lucky to have seen the development of this book from a grain of insight 10 years ago to a complete and comprehensive look at teamwork, leadership, and the limitation of goals. We hope you, the reader, share in our enthusiasm for these ideas. As you read this adventure, you may find yourself rethinking some of your core beliefs and how they may be influencing your actions. If this is the case, then you will achieve what we think the author set out to accomplish in this book—to help you learn from your own experience in order to create new knowledge about the goals you choose to pursue.

Alice and David Kolb
Molokai, Hawaii
March 2006.

Preface

The 1996 Mt Everest climbing disaster, chronicled in a number of books, movies, and television shows, as well as Internet chat rooms the world over, grabbed the interest of climbers and nonclimbers alike. Jon Krakauer's book *Into Thin Air* remained on the best-seller list for over a year.

The world has changed since 1996. The Kingdom of Nepal, the location of the disaster, has seen its tourism business, which boomed in the mid-1990s, drop by nearly half as Maoist insurgents gain influence over most of the country, making it dangerous for many foreigners. The insurgents now claim authority over many districts of the Kingdom. The Everest region of Nepal, the destination of most mountain climbers, and the launching point in Katmandu remain as just a handful of areas out of reach of the insurgency (Douglas, 2005).

The magnitude of the September 11, 2001 events and more recent terrorist attacks in Madrid and London as well as other locations throughout the world has left the world a colder place. A coalition army, led by British and US forces, has staged a protracted war in Iraq, and a series of natural disasters from the southern United States to South Asia have left hundreds of thousands dead or homeless. For many, these events overshadow the tragic deaths of eight mountain climbers on Mt Everest. The events may have moved from the forefront of people's attention, but the events and those involved remain visible, even at the forgetful pace of the new millennium. The story of the 1996 Mt Everest climbing disaster remains compelling, not just for the innocence of the 1990s, but for all times.

The events remain compelling because they provoke questions of the deepest kind. What lengths will a person go just to reach a goal? What is the obligation of a leader to his followers? What is the nature of human desire that pushes some to risk their lives for a few moments on the top of the world? These questions seem heavy enough, but the events provoke questions of another kind as well. How can an organization improve the day-to-day workings of a group of people who share the same goal but fail to see themselves as sharing a common fate? What is the most effective way to pursue a challenging goal? How do you know when to abandon the goal and return another day?

The events that began on May 9, 1996, and continued for the next 72 hours or so remain so compelling not simply because they raise such

questions but, more importantly, because we as observers have failed
to find a satisfying response to these questions. Whether the questions
are philosophical or pragmatic, much about the events, especially an
explanation for what went awry, seems to be as elusive today as it was
in 1996.

With the benefit of retrospect, we can see that the 1996 Everest events
may have foreshadowed some of the key issues of the next few decades.
Some of the basic features of the disaster remain important to the discussion well into the early twenty-first century:

▶ *Globalization*: The multinational teams of climbers needed to manage
diverse cultures to achieve a common goal.
▶ *Relationships between leaders and followers*: The changing nature
of mountain climbing altered the fundamental relationship between
leader and follower.
▶ *Economic inequality*: Low-paid local guides risked their lives to get
rich clients to the top of the mountain. Local Sherpa support personnel
earn about US$6 per day versus the US$65,000 paid by clients to join
an Everest expedition.
▶ *Ethics*: The team leader acted as custodian for the survival of the
organization.

These and other issues remain relevant today, not just in mountain
climbing but in organizations of all kinds. Sherry Ortner, an anthropologist who studies Himalayan culture, nicely summarizes the relevance of
the events for contemporary organizations:

> The public drama of the 1996 Everest fatalities was the result of
> several late-twentieth-century developments. There was first of all the
> growth in communications technology, such that several parties on
> the mountain had the capacity for live communication via computer
> and telephone to any part of the world directly from the mountain
> itself.... A second factor bringing the events to world attention was
> the rise of so-called "adventure travel" in the last decade or so, wherein
> relatively inexperienced individuals pay large sums of money to parti-
> cipate in dangerous sports. (Ortner, 1999, p. 4)

Although these issues remain relevant and important, this book focuses
less on these "global" issues and more on the beliefs and behaviors of
the leaders and followers on Everest and how such beliefs and behaviors
led to the drama that enfolded. It is here, the book contends, in the
day-to-day actions and immediate beliefs of leaders where the real work
of leaders begin. Leadership can be shown not only by taking on the

world's greatest problems but also in leading the world to improved problem solving.

Personal experience in Nepal

In 1996 I visited Nepal as part of a commercial trekking group. I had been struggling with my professional life as a stockbroker and then later a consultant and had decided to make a career change. A hiking trip to Nepal seemed a compelling way to spend a few months prior to pursuing a doctorate in organizational behavior. Nepal offered what I hoped would be a refreshing immersion in Nepalese culture as well as the beautiful natural setting of the Himalayas. In retrospect, I came across one of the most compelling stories about leadership and teams I had ever experienced.

If what I went to do was hike in the natural landscape of the Himalayas, what I stumbled upon was a mystery of human nature. I wrote the following words in the journal *Organizational Dynamics*:

> As I explored the foothills of Mt Everest, one of the world's most tragic mountain-climbing disasters began to unfold on the peak itself. In an unwavering pursuit of the summit, teams ignored pre-established turnaround times. As a result, several teams became lost, and others were too weak to continue down the mountain. During the days following the incident, my colleagues and I, hiking at much more modest heights, came across survivors of that ill-fated expedition.
>
> Troubled by my first-hand encounter with such tragedy, I have spent nearly a decade studying disasters, mishaps, and problems encountered in a variety of organizational settings. I have conducted an extensive analysis of the positive and negative effects of goals, reviewed case studies of goal-setting sessions, spoke with numerous executives and leaders, and executed various studies of my own. In the end, I have concluded that while goals often provide the promise for great leadership and lead us to lofty heights, goals can also steer us to take dangerous chances (Kayes, 2005, p. 391).

The relevance of dilemmas for the study of leadership

After receiving my doctorate, I have used the Everest tragedy to teach principles of leadership to students and business executives. Many participants in these sessions are familiar with the events, since they became the subject of a number of best-selling books, including Jon Krakauer's book *Into Thin Air*, as well as several documentaries.

The tragedy consistently held participants' attention. The nature of the content leads to interesting class conversation and, ultimately, I hope, learning. One day a participant in an MBA program approached me after the session. The student expressed concern that a mountain-climbing disaster was not an appropriate topic for understanding leadership in organizations. This student, of Russian descent, worked at a large electronics manufacturer in Finland and had studied at one of Europe's prestigious business schools. He expressed it this way, which I paraphrase:

> A business person should not study topics filled with such great tragedy and emotion. Tragedy and emotion constitute a different kind of knowledge than what is required of leaders. It hurts the credibility of leaders when we delve into an organization and talk about such tragedy. Questions of tragedy and the dilemmas of human existence should be left to the poet, the novelist, and the playwright. These topics have nothing to do with why we study leadership in organizations.

I did not press the participant to explain any further, but he continued by presenting me with a writing tablet on which he had drawn a $2'' \times 2''$ matrix. The matrix presented his position in a more systematic way. Along one dimension was knowledge; on the other dimension, relevance. Using this graphic, the student demonstrated that, although tragedy was important, it was not relevant to understanding leadership, particularly in a business context. While such tragedy fit into the overall scheme of what should be known, he argued, it is outside the realm of relevance for the leader.

The comments of the student failed to shock me. Over the years of my brief career as a manager, professor, and consultant, I have experienced similar reactions about the appropriateness of studying certain topics in the context of leadership. Many consider tragedy and its concern with death, love, and emotions off limits for leadership discourse. The student's concerns were instructive but not unique. After having used the Mt Everest events for several years to teach about topics such as leadership, team dynamics, and ethical decision-making (see Kayes, 2002a, 2006), I have grown accustomed to questions about the relevance of a mountain-climbing disaster to practicing leaders in more grounded organizations.

This particular student's concerns caught my attention because of the sheer clarity by which the student articulated his position and his sheer resolve that the nature of this topic was inappropriate. He continued: "I know the position I have taken is controversial and surely many in the class will disagree, so I have chosen not to actively participate in this part of the course."

The exchange with this student helped me understand several things about using the events of the 1996 Mt Everest disaster as a tool to help leaders understand the complexity of the situations they face. This book represents an answer to this student and others like him. It provides an explicit and comprehensive analysis of how and why the Everest events, and their ensuing tragedy, deserve a place in the conversation about leadership. The events of 1996 provide, in my experience, one of the most powerful stories of how leaders create and lead through human dilemma. The events can instruct other leaders, working in other circumstances, on the perils of goal-setting gone too far.

The student so brilliantly stated the reverse of a series of questions that I had been asking myself for some time: What if human tragedy served as the context for understanding leadership? What if scholars and practicing leaders understood leadership from the viewpoint of a novelist, as a series of human dilemmas that involve uneasy choices that often result in unsatisfactory outcomes? What if we began to express leadership in the way of the Greek poets, as story that deciphers the complexity of human experience?

This book comes in the form of a response to those people, like my student, who remain skeptical of talking about the tragedy of human experience in the context of leadership. The aim of this book lies in providing a theoretically coherent yet accessible explanation of how leaders experience human dilemma through the events of the 1996 Mt Everest climbing disaster. Here lies the fundamental lesson from Everest: *Learning, not goals, provides the means to resolving leadership's toughest challenges.*

Leaders extol the value of setting and pursuing challenging goals, but when does the process of goal-setting go too far and become destructive? By searching for an answer to this question, this book provides practicing leaders with new insights into how to better utilize the goal-setting process. The tragic events of 1996 vividly illustrate how leaders and team members working on difficult problems in organizations can learn in the face of challenging situations. Through a detailed recounting of events and allusions to contemporary leadership practice, the book shows how:

▶ setting and pursuing high and difficult goals often drive failure, not just success
▶ learning and adaptation, not vision alone, lie at the heart of leadership
▶ effective teamwork and learning, not simply goal-setting, leads to success in the face of novel situations.

A growing body of evidence suggests that setting and pursuing challenging goals leads to disaster as often as success. In a time when people rely on the redemptive power of goals more than ever, this book helps leaders cultivate the positive effects of pursuing goals rather than falling prey to the destructive forces of goals.

Acknowledgements

Like the pursuit of any worthwhile goal, writing a book requires the support of many. I would like to thank my family, Anna, Braden, and Ben for sacrificing long weekends and evenings as I pursued this project. They provided both the inspiration and healthy encouragement during the final push. Ben's birth provided sleepless nights to compile the manuscript and Braden's attempt to explain "goalodicy" to his fourth grade class a source of pride. Anna's support sustained my spirit. I thank my parents, Joan and Kosmas, who have always encouraged the pursuit of ambitious goals, but not at the expense of family and friends.

I thank Stephan Rutt and his crew at Palgrave Macmillan for their support on this project. David and Alice Kolb of Case Western Reserve University have shown support from the first paper I wrote on this topic in 1996. They have provided encouragement, critique, and patience on countless drafts of these ideas over the years. Poppy McCloud, Diana Bilimoria, and Vanessa Druskat all deserve special thanks for the same reasons. Richard Boyatzis and Eric Neilsen, both early supporters of this work, proved a valuable source of intellectual inspiration.

I thank the members of the Department of Management at the George Washington University who have supported challenging conventional wisdom about many things, especially James Bailey, Patrick McHugh, Tjai Nielsen, and Erik Winslow; and Melissa Knott, Craig Seal, Rayshad Holmes, and Nate Allen, Garry Burnett, and Jon Raelin, who continually accept my limitations as a leader. David Schwandt, Marshall Sashkin, and Andrea Casey of the Human and Organizational Studies group, and a group of mentors and collaborators including Russ Vince, Dale Fitzgibbons, David Luechauer, Gordon Dehler, David Stirling, Ted Leahey, and Cynthia Orticio have been instrumental in supporting me as well.

Introduction

This chapter introduces destructive goal pursuit through the story of Bruce Herrod and the South African expedition. It defines the key concepts that appear throughout the book, including destructive goal pursuit, called here *goalodicy*, and the role of leadership in destructive goal pursuit. This chapter presents the three counterintuitive points of the book: the limits of goals and their pursuit, the need for less attention on goals and more attention on group dynamics, and the problems brought about by strong leadership.

Trouble on the South African team

Bruce Herrod, a climber unfamiliar to most save for a few mountain climbers and those interested in the details of the 1996 Mt Everest climbing disaster, suffered the fate of identifying too closely with a goal as yet unachieved. A professional photographer, Herrod joined the 1996 South African expedition team to represent that nation's first attempt to summit the world's tallest peak. Recovering from centuries of apartheid rule, the small nation saw the opportunity to summit Everest as a statement of national identity. A successful summit of Everest would surely make for good headlines around the world.

Ian Woodall headed up the South African expedition. According to some, Woodall's flair for publicity was matched only by the flare of his temper. Even those who had met Woodall briefly called his leadership style "erratic" and referred to him as a "control freak" (Krakauer, 1997a, p. 56). *The Johannesburg Sun Times*, the financial sponsor of the expedition, might have become suspicious of Woodall when it witnessed his unconventional method of recruiting expedition members. Seeking a woman team member, Woodall created an essay contest to identify participants.

The excitement surrounding the expedition and the pride of sponsoring the first South African expedition allowed even *The Johannesburg Sun Times* to overlook such strange behavior. But when it learned that Woodall lied about his prior experience as a mountain climber, the paper fired him. Woodall, however, continued to the summit despite the lost endorsement. Just days into the 1996 expedition, the most experienced members deserted the expedition team, many of them citing Woodall's temper, authoritarian leadership style, and unpredictable demeanor as the reasons for leaving.

1

Herrod, however, chose not to disengage from the South African team. As a struggling freelance photographer and right-hand man to Woodall, Herrod might have believed that reaching the summit of Everest would be a good career move. At the time of his ascent, only about 600 people had ever reached the summit of Everest and returned safely to tell about it. Herrod hoped to return with pictures in hand. It may have been Herrod's knowledge of photography and the expected related publicity that appealed to Woodall (Krakauer, 1997a, p. 163). Also remaining with Woodall was the winner of Woodall's essay contest—Cathy O'Dowd, a relatively experienced climber by South African standards. O'Dowd would recount her first reaction when she heard about the call: "The climbing of Everest had never entered my mind before. It was not a childhood dream, not a life-long ambition. If I had ever thought of it, I had dismissed the idea instantly, as Everest was too big, too far away, too expensive" (O'Dowd, 1999).

Herrod's climb to the summit was probably not pretty. He must have passed the body of American expedition leader Scott Fischer, who had frozen to death 10 days earlier. Herrod had been at the South Col and witnessed the near-death state of Texas pathologist-turned-mountain-climber Beck Weathers, who had cheated death in his summit attempt days before. Herrod helped in their rescue, although other members of his team, including Woodall, refused to lend his radio to the rescue team. Yet, Herrod continued to pursue the summit, despite witnessing horror nearly unimaginable to those of us who reside at lower altitude. Herrod had pursued the summit well into the evening of May 25.

Woodall reported reaching the summit at about 9:30 that morning with O'Dowd right behind but Herrod nowhere to be seen. Some reported that Herrod reached the summit at about 5:30 p.m. and was in contact with the South African team as late as 7:00 p.m. on May 14 (Krakauer, 1997a, p. 163). O'Dowd and Woodall would reach other high points of their lives together. They were married and in 2002 experienced another adventure. In order to escape criminal charges brought against them by tax collectors in the United Kingdom, the two who once stood hand in hand on top of the world's tallest mountain fled to the tax haven of Andorra (Padayachee, 2002). Herrod reached the summit but never returned to base camp. He was one of 15 people to die on Everest that season, the worst toll in the 50 years since Everest was first conquered in 1953.

By most accounts, the South African expedition resulted in a fiasco. That the expedition ultimately failed is not surprising since it appears to embody most or all of the elements of overpursuing a goal. Other expedition teams also experienced extraordinary failure that season. Unlike the South African team, however, these other teams were composed of experienced, visionary, and transformational leaders, experienced climbers with seemingly right motives: achieving ambitious goals, setting their sights high, and working together to achieve these goals. Yet, several of the experienced expedition teams experienced the same grim consequences as the less savvy South African team. The experienced Everest teams failed, despite possessing many of the factors thought related to successful goal achievement, such as strong leadership, collective team efforts, and focused goal-setting.

For example, two other expedition leaders who died that season were among the best leaders on the mountain. Many considered Rob Hall and Scott Fischer the strongest and most trusted guides. Each achieved their trust through the successes and failures that result only from years of climbing. Both guides achieved records of successful summits, but both were prone to making grandiose and inaccurate claims of their climbing feats. Hall, a New Zealander, who had advertised his 100 percent rate of success on Everest, had nonetheless failed to get all his clients to the top the prior year. The prior season failure may have made him overly anxious to help certain clients attain their dreams. Likewise, Fischer would claim that his success on Everest had become routine—or, as he stated, "We've got the big 'E' [Everest] all figured out"—despite experiencing several unacknowledged setbacks during the 1996 season. These and other proclamations by team leaders and team members signal the fact that many important details essential for successful climbing may have been overlooked in narrow-minded pursuit of the summit.

Search for answers

This book begins with the experience of Herrod because it calls attention to the central question posed by this book: Why would a leader continue to pursue a goal despite mounting evidence it could not be obtained? In their unwavering pursuit of the summit, why did so many climbers ignore pre-established turnaround times and continue to the summit? Herrod's ascent provides some insight into one of the most pressing problems faced by leaders: when to abandon a goal, despite having invested much effort into its pursuit. A better understanding of Herrod's motivations and how he viewed goals may provide insight into dilemmas faced by other leaders. A better understanding of mountain climbers like those on Everest might lead us to a better understanding of leaders working at less lofty heights as well (Mitchell, 1983).

This book explores some possible explanations for the behavior of Herrod and others who continued up the mountain that season. The book reviews research on leadership, management, and organizations for an explanation as well as analysis of the events themselves from the perspective of leadership (Digenti, 2001; Useem, 2001). In the end, however, existing explanations, while they provide insight, remain incomplete. A look at the events in terms of the limits of goal-setting might lead to a different conclusion about what occurred on Everest. The conclusion considers one of the least-understood areas of leadership: how goals shape the identity of leaders and their followers. The explanation put forth in this book about why the leaders and their groups pursue goals to their own detriment exposes a limitation in our understanding of the leadership process. More specifically, the events expose a problem with the goal-setting process and how goals may actually limit the intended work of leaders. The limits of leadership arise from destructive goal pursuit, a process this book calls *goalodicy* (Kayes, 2004b).

This book seeks to learn from the stories of Herrod and others like him who have not cowered from lofty goals but have been lured into destruction by their passion for goals. Herrod's story seems a good place to start this learning because his passion and abilities as a climber were not suspect. Herrod was an experienced and strong expedition team member. After all, the Royal Geographic Society named Herrod a Fellow back in 1978 for his successful expeditions. We might turn to the Society's obituary for insight. It remembered that "As his portfolio [of successful expeditions] increased so did his passion for the mountains . . . but he always seemed to burden himself with too much weight of photographic equipment" (Colin, 1996, pp. 360–361). So it is with goals. As men and women seek ever higher and more ambitious goals, the weight of their pursuit becomes ever more burdensome. In a time when people rely on the redemptive power of goals more than ever, this book suggests a way to cultivate the positive effects of pursuing goals rather than falling prey to the destructive forces of goalodicy.

Goalodicy is not just a problem with mountain climbers or those engaged in setting uncommonly ambitious goals. Goalodicy describes one of the most pressing dilemmas faced by leaders in organizations: When should a leader abandon a pre-established goal and regroup?

Organizational leaders and scholars alike advocate setting and pursuing ambitious goals. The unquestionable value of goal-setting has become ingrained in the culture of organizations. Goals have become the theology of contemporary leadership; evidence to support their effectiveness is abundant. Oddly, with all the interest in goals, only a handful of studies have focused on the limits of goals and their unintended consequences. In order to be effective in the face of increasingly complex problems, leaders need a better understanding of the limits, as well as the benefits, of goal-setting (Kayes, 2005).

Through a detailed recounting of events and allusions to teams working in other goal-directed endeavors, this book argues three main points.

1. Setting and pursuing high and difficult goals often drive failure.
The Everest team leaders thought they "had it all figured out" when, in fact, meeting the challenge of summiting the world's highest mountain still required learning new things. There is need among leaders to distinguish between tasks that require learning strategies and those that require performance-driven strategies. This book will show that setting high goals under conditions that require learning often drives failure. For example, Herrod met his goal of achieving the summit yet fell victim to an unintended consequence of his goal: failing to make it back down.

2. Learning and adaptation, not vision alone, lie at the heart of leadership.
Several of the leaders on Everest relied on authoritarian leadership styles to motivate and organize their teams. This approach led to team members who could not make decisions on their own. Leadership requires developing team members as much as dictating actions, and such development can be stifled in dependent relationships. Herrod, like many other climbers on Everest, likely fell victim to his leader's ambitions and became so dependent on his leader that he may have become unable to make effective decisions once he ventured alone.

3. Effective teamwork and learning, not simply goal-setting, lead to success in the face of novel situations.
The Everest leaders virtually ignored teamwork as a necessary component of success. The leaders took for granted that people had the necessary interpersonal skills to succeed. Mountain climbing, like leadership, evokes images of lone, individual climbers achieving nearly superhuman accomplishments when, in reality, most climbing is done in teams. By its very nature, teamwork increases the complexity of problem solving by introducing a host of psychological and sociological dynamics. Herrod began his ascent as part of a team yet reached the peak and ultimately failed alone. Herrod's strategy may have been the correct one; however, without the support and experience of a group, he ultimately was unable to realize the fruits of his success. He realized the unfortunate and unintended consequence of not getting back down.

Drawing on systematic research, recounting stories from mountain climbing, and exploring teams engaged in a variety of activities, the following chapters will illustrate how these misconceptions about leadership can lead to unfortunate, even tragic, consequences in organizations. The book describes the consequences of goalodicy and provides a path to avoid them in the pursuit of ambitious projects. A summary of the problem of goalodicy, including warnings, causes, and potential ways to overcome goalodicy, is presented in the box below.

SUMMARY OF GOALODICY

Goalodicy

A situation in which the normally helpful process of goal-setting becomes dysfunctional; the effort put toward achieving a goal results in unintended consequences:

- ▶ **A breakdown of teamwork**
- ▶ **A breakdown of learning**
- ▶ **Difficulty abandoning goals, even when they may result in disaster**
- ▶ **Unethical decisions**
- ▶ **Excessive risk-taking**
- ▶ **Inability to accomplish goal.**

Warning signs

- ▶ **A narrowly defined goal**
- ▶ **A prevailing public expectation that achieving the goal is imminent**
- ▶ **Face-saving behavior displayed by the team or individual**
- ▶ **The idealization of a future with no or few problems**
- ▶ **Pursuit that is justified by the goal itself and not other logic**
- ▶ **The feeling, shared among team members, that achieving the goal is destiny.**

Causes

- ▶ **Identification with a distant, idealized, or narrow goal**
- ▶ **Dependence on a leader or leaders for key decisions**
- ▶ **Emergence of a novel, complex situation requiring critical thinking and problem solving.**

Remedies

- ▶ **Recognizing ill-structured problems**
- ▶ **Learning from experience**
- ▶ **Engaging in recovery**
- ▶ **Fostering trust**
- ▶ **Developing tacit coordination**
- ▶ **Minding the gap**
- ▶ **Cultivating multiple goals.**

Organization of the book

One criticism of using the Everest events to show the realities of leadership is "Why would someone want to climb a mountain anyway?" This question inevitably leads many to discount the events as involving a bunch of extremists and to discount the relevance of the lessons for more common organizations. The inclusion of short vignettes to introduce the central chapters of this book serves as a response to these critics by showing how destructive goal pursuit takes hold. These vignettes are fiction but rely heavily on my own experience in the Himalayas as well as accounts by high altitude mountain climbers. These vignettes should help readers understand the *experience* of goalodicy from outset to onset.

The book is divided into four main parts

Part I: Learning from the Everest Disaster draws on the Everest disaster to illustrate how leaders can fall prey to destructive goal pursuit. Part I recounts the tragic events of Everest. It reviews the various explanations put forth for the events and exposes the weakness of each. These explanations have included the ambitions and actions of leaders, dysfunctional group processes, and the inexperience of climbers. While each reason helps explain events, each in and of itself is incomplete. Destructive goal pursuit provides a more complete and detailed explanation of the events.

Part II: Destructive Goal Pursuit delves into what went wrong on Everest at various levels. After defining and explaining goalodicy and highlighting four limits of goals, it examines how destructive goal pursuit was facilitated by elements of leadership and by the breakdown of learning in teams. The part also identifies warning signs of goalodicy: a narrowly defined goal, public expectation, face-saving behavior, an idealized future, goal-driven justification, and achieving destiny. Finally, the part brings together many of the factors and presents a seven-stage process for how goalodicy can develop.

Part III: From Destructive to Productive Pursuit moves from explaining events to providing guidance on ways to cultivate the positive effects of goals. Drawing on lessons from the survival and eventual rescue of climbers on Everest, as well as from military expeditions and other action teams, the part offers insight into why *teamwork* is important for defining and achieving most goals and how *team learning* proves essential in the face of novel situations. Team learning can occur even when immediate response is required; the TArT model of learning is presented for this environment. Seven specific remedies are given for overcoming destructive pursuit of goals.

Part IV: Rethinking Leadership in Organizations challenges the notion that goal-setting involves simply a systematic and rational process. The book describes goal-setting as a challenging process of managing multiple goals and obligations. Part IV integrates the previous parts into a useful and thought-provoking approach to leadership in light of the difficulties of the goal-setting process.

This part recommends a number of remedies to destructive goal pursuit. The recipe suggests that leaders must acknowledge setbacks, adapt, and re-evaluate goals. Abandoning goals does not come easy, but failing to abandon goals comes with costs of its own.

Leaders face many challenges relative to goals. Whether leaders serve in extreme situations like Everest or in more typical organizations, they must balance individual and team goals, recognize unintended consequences that emerge from goal pursuit, and battle the disappointments that inevitably emerge when goals need to be abandoned. All the while, leaders must continually recognize the ethical demands that present themselves during goal pursuit. Understanding how teams work and more importantly how they learn becomes the first step in overcoming destructive goal pursuit.

Part I Learning from the Everest Disaster

1 The 1996 Mount Everest Climbing Disaster: Recounting the Tragic Events

Imagine training your sights on a distant goal, an ideal dream. You devote resources, make sacrifices, and direct unwavering attention to achieving the goal. The goal may have begun as a dream, like climbing a mountain. The lure of mountaineering is magical. After a few successful climbs on short, easy routes, you seek greater challenges. Dreaming of the summit becomes electric, the experience of climbing a craving. After a time your dreams become bigger. Each mountain peak you climb and each successful summit make you crave more. You begin to catch what climbers call "summit fever."

Each summit attempt makes you better than the last. You gain skill, knowledge, and ability. Literally, you learn the ropes of climbing. You learn how to depend on your partners, and you learn to depend on yourself. You learn to read the warning signs of bad weather. You may become more cautious, or you may become bold. Whatever experiences you gather, these feelings only increase the intensity of the climb. Your day job becomes less interesting. The lure of the summit, the sweaty palms that accompany summit fever, trump the routine of the office cubicle.

You find yourself taking more time off from work. What was once a small hobby begins to consume more of you to the disappointment but excitement of family, friends, and coworkers. Many begin to feel cheated by your new love. At the same time, you see yourself taking on a new status. Friends listen in amazement to your stories of triumph and defeat. As others observe the thrill of sport from the comforts of the couch, you are living it. The weekend golfers burrow in comparison to your stories. Your friends ask you about the latest climb and what peak you plan to "bag" next. They may have read a story about Everest and kid you about when you "plan to bag the big one." Your distant dream takes on a social life of its own.

If you have the privilege of a large disposable income, you begin to acquire the latest climbing gear. You read about the latest developments in materials, the latest designs and features in the adventure magazines that litter your home. Tags with names like "The North Face" and "Mountain Hardware" show up on your gear and clothes. You begin to pour more and more money

into your passion. Traveling to remote parts of the world requires resources.
Even the used equipment that you buy drains your cash. You have to pay for
the services of a guide, and that's expensive too. If you live on a fixed income,
you may find yourself taking out loans to pay the fees to bag even bigger and
more exotic peaks. While you may dream of someday leaving behind your day
job to pursue climbing full time, you know that only a handful of the most elite
climbers ever gain enough sponsorships to pay all the bills.

Regardless of your financial status, you become entranced by the love,
the history, the mythology of climbing. Your leisure reading takes form in
stories about mountain climbing. You read High Adventure, *the personal*
account of Sir Edmund Hillary. You're likely to read Seven Summits *by*
businessman Dick Bass, who recounts how he successfully climbed the tallest
summits on each of the world's seven continents. You also read about the
tragic climbs, such as the failed 1982 expedition of Marty Hoey, the first
American woman to attempt the summit.

The stories you tell, the things you read, the people with whom you identify:
what begins as a simple activity becomes a lifestyle. You join, consciously
or not, the "brotherhood and sisterhood of the rope," the informal term for
serious and dedicated climbers. You have become part of a culture—the
culture of mountain climbing.

Like the avid golfer, who wears golf shirts to work and dreams of playing
the old course at St. Andrew's, you become entranced with the symbols of
your culture and dream of bagging "the big one," Everest. It gives you a
place in history and a place in the social order. If golf is a game of inches, so
is climbing. Unlike golf, however, the consequences of those inches are much
greater on the rope than in the bunker. Others begin to see you as a different
sort. The golfers especially see you as crazy. But this only reinforces your goal,
since not everyone else is doing it.

This is the context in which you begin to see your distant goal, summiting
Everest, transformed into experience. You take notice of the ads in adventure
magazines looking for climbers to join the next Everest expedition. What
began as a dream, manifesting itself in a casual jib at the water cooler, is
now a goal within your reach. Long ignored is the fate of men and women
who identify too closely with a goal as yet unachieved.[1]

The events surrounding the 1996 Mt Everest climbing season remain alive
in books, Internet chat rooms, popular media, and, most importantly, the
lore of mountain climbers. The events themselves have spurred numerous
books from survivors and several popular press accounts. The events and

---

[1] Chapter introductions are fictionalized accounts that illustrate the experience of destructive
goal pursuit. The introductions are fictional but are based on the author's experience hiking in
the Himalayas as well as accounts of high altitude mountain climbers.

people provide particularly ripe material for understanding the successes and failures of leaders pursuing goals. The disaster has served as the source of articles, case studies, and classroom exercises designed to help managers and students navigate the challenging terrain of complex problems. The events have been retold countless times, and this chapter provides new insight by looking at the people and events in light of the destructive pursuit of goals.

This chapter recounts the events by piecing together published memoirs of survivor recollections and popular press reports. While a total of 15 climbers died on the mountain in 1996, this analysis focuses on the deaths of 8 climbers from three teams. The missteps of these leaders and followers and their dramatic rescue provide ample details to consider the substance of destructive goal pursuit. This book will eventually venture beyond the limits of the 1996 events, but for now the chapter focuses only on the brief history of climbing Mt Everest and the impact of this history on the 1996 expeditions.

History of climbing Everest

The British confirmed Mt Everest as the highest point in the world in 1852 and named the mountain after Sir George Everest, the head of the Great Trigonometrical Survey of India. The group of people native to the Everest region, the Sherpas, live in the foothills that surround Everest and call the mountain Chomolungma, which translates roughly to "mother goddess of earth" (Ortner, 1999, p. 26).

Not until 1921 was an expedition made to the summit of Everest. George Mallory launched the first well-funded expedition to reach the summit. Mallory tried to reach the summit three times. On his third try, he died. The controversy as to whether or not Mallory or his climbing partner Irvine made it to the top continues to this day. Even the discovery of Mallory's body and some of his gear in 1999 has not answered the question of whether Mallory made it to the top and died on his way down (visit PBS Online, 2000).

No one had reached the summit and lived to tell about it until New Zealand beekeeper Edmond Hillary and Sherpa expedition expert Tenzing Norgay successfully reached the summit at 11:30 a.m. on May 29, 1953 and returned back safely. Over the next 50 years, nearly 1,200 climbers from 63 nations reached the summit of Everest. These successes came at a cost, however. Reports confirm that 175 deaths occurred in the same 50 years (Miller, 2003).

One of the early signs of change on the mountain came when an ambitious American climber named Eric Simonson successfully guided 10 paying clients to the top and down safely in the early 1990s. According to some, the success of Simonson in leading this group of paying climbers to the top of the mountain signaled a changing tide in Everest expeditions: paying clients became followers, and paid guides became leaders. Rather than the prevailing interdependent relationship among team members, an economic relationship had developed (Elmes and Barry, 1999). These changes may have set the stage for 1996, the worst year in the nearly 50-year history of climbing Everest. Table 1 summarizes the key participants in 1996 and other important people mentioned throughout the book.

Table 1 **Summary of participants**

American Team Members (a.k.a. Mountain Madness)

Fischer, Scott	Team leader, experienced at altitude, died on descent.
Beidleman, Neal	Assistant guide to Scott Fischer, assisted clients in ascent and descent from summit.
Boukreev, Anatoli	Assistant guide to Fischer, summited without oxygen, risked own life to save Pittman, Madsen, and Fox.
Fox, Charlotte	Client, climbing with partner Tim Madson.
Hill Pittman, Sandy	Client, socialite, relatively experienced climber, was "short roped" to the summit by Fischer's assistant guide Jangbu.
Jangbu, Lopsang	Head Sherpa and assistant guide to Fischer, criticized for "short roping" Pittman to summit and failing to help other Sherpas set climbing ropes on summit day.
Madson, Tim	Client, climbing with partner Charlotte Fox.

New Zealand Team Members (a.k.a. Adventure Consultants)

Hall, Rob	Team leader, experienced guide with strong will, died on descent while helping Hansen.
Groom, Mike	Assistant guide to Rob Hall, helped bring back group of climbers on descent.
Hansen, Doug	Client, in 1995, Hall turned Hansen around a few hundred feet from the summit, died in 1996 after reaching summit.
Harris, Andy "Harold"	Assistant guide to Hall. Died after reaching the summit.
Kasischke, Lou	Client, turned around at 11:00 a.m. after realizing he could not reach the summit.
Krakauer, Jon	Client, journalist reporting on commercialization of Everest for *Outside* Magazine. Wrote best-selling book based on his account "Into Thin Air."
Namba, Yasuka	Client, Japanese climber died a few hundred yards from Camp IV after reaching summit.
Weathers, Beck	Client, unable to continue pursuit of the summit, returned after waiting hours in the cold. Left for dead twice by rescue party, descended to high camp on his own effort and survived.

Table I **continued**

Taiwanese Team Members

Gau, Makalu	Team leader, left Chen to fend for himself after Chen's fall and nearly died himself on descent.
Chen Yu-nan	Died after taking a fall after carelessly walking out of camp without boots.

South African Team Members (a.k.a. Johannesburg Sunday Times Expedition)

Herrod, Bruce	Adventurer, photographer, reached summit at 5:00 and died on descent.
O'Dowd, Cathy	Became only female member of team after winning an essay contest on why she wanted to summit Everest.
Woodall, Ian	Controversial team leader, called a "control freak," alienates team members who quit the expedition, only O'Dowd and Herrod remain.

Members of Rescue Party

Burleson, Todd	Leader of Alpine Ascents team, experienced climber who organizes rescue at Camp IV.
Athans, Peter	Experienced climber and member of Alpine Ascents team, organizes rescue from Camp IV.
Breashears, David	Experienced climber and high altitude film maker, leader of the Everest IMAX team.
Madan, Colonel	Nepalese helicopter pilot who risked his life to shuttle ailing climbers Weathers and Gau to safety.
Viesturs, Ed	The most accomplished US climber. His early decision to delay his summit attempt foreshadows disaster.

Other climbers mentioned

Bass, Dick	Texas businessman whose book "The Seven Summits" is thought to usher in commercial climbing on Everest.
Bonington, Chris	Experienced climber and writer, he is known for his personal written accounts of mastering difficult peaks.
Hillary, Edmund	Member of first team to summit Everest, along with Tenzing Norgay.
Norgay, Tenzing	Member of first successful Everest summit along with Hillary.
Hoey, Marty	First American female to attempt Everest, suffered fatal fall.
Mallory, George	Early Everest pioneer, debate still continues if he and climbing partner Irvine actually reached summit in 1921.
Irvine, Andrew	Climbing partner of George Mallory.
Messner, Reinhold	First individual to summit Everest without supplemental bottled oxygen.
Simonson, Eric	Led one of the most visible and successful early commercial expeditions to Everest.

The guides

Among his many distinguishing physical features, Rob Hall was uncommonly tall for a mountain climber. His deep-set eyes, square face, and heavy but trim beard created a mythic hero quality about his presence. He resembled the American folk hero Paul Bunyan, the oversized lumberjack who created the American Grand Canyon by dragging his axe across the ground. Hall projected the kind of confidence, strength, and trustworthiness that followers often seek in their leaders. He built his reputation as a trustworthy and competent Everest guide on more than his appearance. He had cut his teeth in New Zealand, his home country, and in several successful climbs around the world's highest peaks. Hall often boasted about his "100 percent success rate" in getting clients to the summit of Everest, even though the 100 percent figure was an exaggeration.

Rob Hall and climbing leader Scott Fischer had growing reputations among climbers as the most successful expedition leaders anywhere. Like Hall, Fischer would also be guiding a group of paying clients to the summit of Everest in 1996. Fischer and Hall became rivals of sorts. Both fought for the small but growing number of clients willing to pay the huge fee and risk their lives for a chance to join the elite group of people who can say they stood at the top of the world, if only for a few minutes. Only a handful of potential clients came with the combination of will, experience, and money to attempt Everest. Any client carrying a resume with this combination proved to be demanding, achievement oriented, and, most of all, goal directed. Fischer and Hall were among the few leaders with the skills and experience to organize large commercial expeditions. Among mountain climbers, there was a growing lore that getting an experienced guide such as Hall or Fischer was an essential element to getting to the summit.

Based on their past successes, both guides deserved their positive reputations. Fischer in particular became a kind of living legend among mountain climbers. A few years earlier, Fischer had participated in a rescue effort on K2, the world's second highest peak. Even though K2 rests a mere 785 feet lower than Everest, most experts consider K2 a more technically difficult climb than Everest. Earlier in the climb, Fischer fell into a crevice and injured his arm. In his final camp at about 24,000 feet, Fischer and his partner, American climber Ed Viesturs, received a call on their radio from French climber Chantel Mauduit. Mauduit and her partners had successfully reached the summit. However, they became trapped in a blinding storm just after beginning their descent. In a daring rescue, Fischer and Viesturs reached the stranded party but only after surviving a nearly calamitous avalanche that would have hurled anyone but the most cautious climbers down the mountain in a wave of snow. Once

Viesturs and Fischer reached the exhausted climbers, they persevered for three agonizing days to bring the three ailing climbers to safety. After the rescue, which would have broken the spirits and weakened the bodies of most climbers, Fischer and Viesturs turned around and successfully reached the summit a few days later.

Fischer's efforts became the stuff of mountain-climbing lore, and he became a celebrity within the mountain-climbing community. If Hall played the dashing leader, Fischer played the consummate adventure guide, best buddy, and competent outdoorsman. The casual observer might see Fischer at home with a surfboard on the beach rather than in a tent on the mountain. Fischer, however, represented a growing kind of archetype in the adventure travel community: the outdoor guide and enthusiast. His long blond ponytail suggested that Fischer had dropped out of the mainstream years ago. Fischer appeared more at home in the unstructured world of adventure climbing than in any organized group. Only recently did Fischer put himself into a position to view his passion for the mountains as a money-making venture.

The climbers

Mountain climbers share some characteristics of hopeless romantics. The hopeless romantic seeks to fulfill desires by engaging in serial romances and then tallying them up. The tally serves to preserve emotions. The illogical experience then becomes chronicled in a logical and systematic way. Climbers share this desire to preserve the fleeting experience by counting the mountains. One popular tally among climbers was reaching the highest peaks on each of the seven continents—a feat first chronicled in the book *Seven Summits* by Dick Bass, a successful Texas businessman turned mountain climber. Bass' account inspired a new breed of climber—one content not by counting any old summit but only by bagging the top peaks.

Seven Summits is significant because it signaled the emergence of not only a new class of climber, but also a new market for climbing guides. Many of those within the climbing community contend that this new breed of "hack" climbers, represented by the likes of Bass, put themselves and others at risk because they exceed their ability and experience. While these hack climbers provide a new market for climbing guides, they pose a threat to the identity of climbers. What does it mean if a rich, middle-aged office dweller like Dick Bass can summit each continent's highest mountain?

Hall's Adventure Consultants team consisted of 24 members: 11 Sherpa climbers and support staff, 5 English-speaking guides, and 8 clients.

Hall's assemblage of paying clients included Beck Weathers, a patholo-
gist who was on a quest to climb the seven summits. By most accounts,
Weathers was not one of the most experienced climbers on the mountain that season, but neither was he just a climbing hack. Among the
more well-known clients on Hall's team, Jon Krakauer had spent many
years climbing technically difficult peaks around the world and writing
about his adventures. If Hall played the part of authoritarian leader
blinded to his own limitations, Krakauer played the part of the Greek
chorus, recounting events to an anxious public, waiting for details of
the fall.

Fischer's Mountain Madness team had 23 members: 10 Sherpa support
staff, 4 English-speaking guides, and 9 clients. Fischer's team included
the high-profile client Sandy Hill Pittman. Hill Pittman possessed the
background that a new enterprise like Mountain Madness would die for.
She was once the wife of MTV founder and media executive Bob Pittman.
The pair was fodder for tabloids, who once called them the "couple of
the minute." She socialized with the likes of TV star Martha Stewart
and news anchor Tom Brokaw. Hill Pittman's climbing ambitions gained
pre-Everest publicity for Fischer's group with an article in the women's
fashion magazine *Vogue*, which chronicled her pre-Everest shopping spree
that included an espresso maker. The year 1996 marked her third attempt
at the summit.

Another notable member of Fischer's team was Klev Schoening, a
relatively inexperienced climber, and his uncle Pete Schoening, at 68 a
legendary climber who had reached each of the highest peaks in the
world, except Everest.

In all, over 16 teams, representing over 300 climbers, support staff,
and observers, arrived at base camp in April 1996 to bid for the summit
in early May.

Push for the summit

After six weeks of acclimatizing and preparing, the Adventure Consultants and Mountain Madness teams were set for the final long push
to the summit of Everest. In his account of the events, climber Jon
Krakauer (1997a) explained that during the final 18-hour push to the
summit, "Survival is to no small degree, a race against the clock"
(p. 173). On May 9, the two teams arrived at Camp IV and began this
race.

If climbers leave Camp IV at 25,938 feet above sea level at 12:00 a.m.,
they should reach the summit between 12:00 and 1:00 p.m. and head
down soon after. Most climbing groups establish turnaround times, or

pre-established times when the climbers must give up their ascent and begin to head down. Past Everest expeditions have agreed on turn-around times that range from a conservative 12:00 p.m. to a risky 2:00 p.m. In an interview conducted after the events, one member of Hall's team reported that Hall established a preferred turnaround time.

On May 9, 1996, at 11:35 p.m. Nepal time, 15 Adventure Consultants team members, including leader Rob Hall and two assistants, Michael Groom and Andy Harris, left Camp IV for the summit. Twelve Mountain Madness team members followed at 12:00 a.m. on May 10, led by assistant leaders Neil Beidleman and Anatoli Boukreev. Team leader Scott Fischer left after his team, sometime between 12:00 and 1:00 a.m. Gau Ming Ho, the leader of a Taiwanese team, left Camp IV soon after with three Sherpa guides. Gau became known by a name he had given himself, Makalu, after an attempt to summit a mountain by the same name. Gau ascended without his climbing partner, Chen Yu-nan, who had died just days earlier. With Gau and what remained of his party, a total of 34 climbers were attempting to summit. By attempting to summit on May 10, Gau broke an agreement made between expedition teams at base camp that only Fischer's and Hall's teams would summit that day (Krakauer, 1997a, p. 155).

While some guides carried two-way radios, most team members did not, and some suggested the radios were inadequate for the task anyway (Boukreev and DeWalt, 1997). Nor did the team members tie themselves together with ropes in case of a fall, as is customary on difficult climbs. Instead, the teams used fixed ropes, which are attached directly to supports on the mountain like rocks and ice. When climbers use fixed ropes, they clip a small mechanism called an ascender onto the rope. The ascenders attach to the climbers' secured harnesses and also grip the rope. The climbers grip the ascender with their hand and slide the ascender along the rope so that they can slide up the rope, similar to a cable car attached to a pulley. The ascender allows the climbers to go up the rope but does not allow them to unexpectedly slide back down. Fixed ropes eliminate the need for climbers to depend on one another for support. Most team members were equipped with individual support technology such as supplementary bottled oxygen and emergency steroid shots.

At about 5:30 a.m., three members of the Mountain Madness team reached the beginning of a long narrow ridge that runs between 27,200 and 28,000 feet called the Southeast Ridge Balcony (Krakauer, 1997a). The teams could not progress up the mountain because fixed safety ropes had not been secured. Soon after, the Adventure Consultants, Mountain Madness, and Taiwanese teams became intermingled at the balcony (Kennedy, 1996), creating the first of several bottlenecks during the climb. The teams worked to fix the ropes and slowly ascended along the balcony between 8:00 and 10:00 a.m. (Kennedy, 1996; Krakauer, 1997a).

Traffic jam at the summit

Between 11:00 and 12:00 p.m., another bottleneck occurred at a 40-foot stretch of rock known as the Hillary Step. The step marks one of the most difficult sections of the climb at 28,800 feet, a mere 250 feet short of the summit. The bottleneck occurred because again, teams had failed to fix ropes as planned. This queue of climbers waiting their turn to ascend the world's tallest peak has become known as the traffic jam. At about 11:40 a.m., two members of the Mountain Madness team and two members of the Adventure Consultants team began to fix ropes (Krakauer, 1997a).

There are conflicting accounts of when various climbers reached the summit; however, somewhere between 1:12 and 1:25 p.m., eight members of the Adventure Consultants and Mountain Madness teams reached the summit, followed shortly by two more Mountain Madness team members. A photograph taken by Fischer at about 2:00 p.m. and retrieved from his camera shows a traffic jam of climbers headed up the final few hundred yards to the summit. The picture shows little evidence of an impending storm, just a few wisps of snow among the climbers. Several more members of each team arrived at the summit between 2:00 and 2:15 p.m. (Kennedy, 1996, p. 148), and several more at about 3:00 p.m., including Gau. At about 3:30 p.m., members of both teams continued to summit. Fischer radioed that all his clients had now reached the summit and were now heading down. He radioed at 3:40 p.m., more than an hour and a half after the absolute latest turnaround time. Doug Hansen, one of Hall's clients, reached the summit just after 4:00 p.m.

The descent

Somewhere between 4:00 and 5:00 p.m., things started to go wrong. One of Fischer's pictures reveals climbers descending into grey clouds. The growing storm soon engulfed the mountain and slowed the descent to a near halt. Climbers equipped for only 18 hours of climbing ran out of bottled oxygen and fatigued quickly without the supplemental support. Some injected the steroids (Kennedy, 1996). Two members of Mountain Madness, including Fischer, and at least two members of Adventure Consultants, including Hall and one of his followers, Doug Hansen, struggled through the storm near the top of the mountain. The whereabouts of assistant leader Harris were unknown. The large number of climbers struggled one by one down the fixed ropes, slowing progress down considerably.

Between 5:00 and 5:20 p.m., assistant leader Beidleman assumed leadership for a group of eight climbers from both teams. At 27,600 feet, this group met Adventure Consultants team member Beck Weathers shivering in the cold. Weathers, who aborted his summit bid 10 hours earlier when his vision became severely impaired at altitude, had been instructed by Hall to stay still until he returned on his descent. Realizing that Hall would not return soon, Weathers joined Beidleman's group on descent. Hall radioed down to support camp for help at 5:00 p.m., saying that he was having trouble getting Hansen down and desperately needed supplementary oxygen.

The huddle

Meanwhile, several other members of both teams arrived back at Camp IV between 4:30 and 6:00 p.m. After getting caught in an earlier bottleneck of climbers, they had turned back at about 11:30 a.m. (Kennedy, 1996, p. 105) and gave up their summit attempt, as the destination was still several hours out of reach.

By 8:00 p.m., the group now led by Beidleman reached the South Col, about 350 yards from Camp IV, but became lost in a fierce storm. Unable to locate camp in near-blinding snow, group members forced each other to stay awake in double-digit subzero wind chill by forming a tight human barrier against the wind and cold in what has become known as the huddle. At about 12:00 a.m. on May 11, a clearing in the clouds allowed Beidleman and Klev Schoening, one of the more experienced clients, to recognize the Big Dipper, as well as the Everest peak itself. These markers allowed them to navigate the short distance to Camp IV. Beidleman, Schoening and Groom navigate their way back to Camp IV and collapse in their tents, but not before giving instructions to Boukreev on the whereabouts of the remaining members of the huddle. Boukreev retrieved all but Nambu and Weathers, who were both believed to be dead. Later the next day, Dr Stuart Hutchison, who had abandon his summit attempt the day before, ventured out to confirm that Namba and Weathers were dead. He found them breathing but confirmed they were too sick to be saved. Weathers' wife was informed that he was dead.

Rescue attempts

Boukreev attempted to organize a search party to reach Fischer but turned back in the storm. At 8:30 a.m., three teams of Sherpas headed out to find the remaining climbers. Hall, trapped near the summit, had been in radio contact through the night and reported that Hansen could not continue down the mountain. At about 10:00 a.m., the Sherpas reached Fischer and Gau about an hour from high camp but were unable to rouse Fischer. The team left Fischer a supply of oxygen and then bundled him. Pulling Gau behind them, a difficult and dangerous act at high altitude, they returned to Camp IV. Weathers, left for dead a second time, amazingly regained consciousness and stumbled into camp completely on his own effort at 4:30 p.m. (Coburn, 1997). Pete Athans and Todd Burleson of the Alpine Ascents, another expedition, had just reached Camp III. Once they heard of the disaster, they abandoned their own expedition and immediately climbed up to Camp IV where the returned climbers were lying. They began offering oxygen and brewing tea.

Attempts to rescue Hall were aborted due to the weather. At 6:40 p.m., Hall, who was still conscious, was patched through by satellite phone for his final dispatch to his wife in New Zealand. He had remained at 28,700 feet for more than 24 hours, frostbitten, without oxygen, and unable to move. Members of other expedition teams, including David Breashears and Ed Viesturs of the IMAX team, assisted in getting Weathers and Gau down the mountain. Weathers would later refer to this as the "dream team" of mountain climbing based on his respect for their mountain-climbing abilities (Breashears, 1999).

In a stunning and never-before-attempted high-altitude rescue, Colonel Madan K. C. of the Nepalese Air Force touched down at over 21,000 feet using a makeshift landing pad marked with Kool-Aid. The pilot retrieved and relocated Gau to lower elevation only to return 45 minutes later to retrieve Weathers.

Among the three teams, eight people died, including three guides, Hall, Fischer, and Harris, and climbers Hansen and Namba, as well as a Taiwanese climber who died earlier in the expedition. Two Sherpa guides were killed, one during an earlier accident and one during the rescue attempt. Additionally, five climbers from other expeditions also died that season, including Bruce Herrod, a member of a South African team who reached the summit at 5:00 p.m. on May 25. Gau and Weathers had such severe frostbite that they lost extremities; Weathers also lost his nose. What happened to Harris has not been clearly established. Krakauer (1997b) suggests he may have become trapped near the summit assisting Hall and Hansen. Table 2 provides a chronology of important events

Table 2 **Chronology of events**

	Date and Time	Key Event	Elevation
①	**May 9** 11:35 p.m	Adventure Consultants and Mountain Madness Teams begin ascent. Taiwanese team follows.	25,900
②	**May 10** 5:30 a.m.	Team members begin to reach Southeast Ridge Balcony. First bottleneck of climbers develops	27,000–28,000
③	8:00–10:00 a.m.	Teams make their way up the balcony	
④	11:00–12:00 a.m.	Second bottleneck at Hilary Step	28,800
	11:30 a.m.	Three members of Adventure Consultant teams abandon summit attempt	
	1:00 p.m	**Typical turnaround time**	
⑤	1:00–1:25 p.m	Eight climbers from Adventure Consultants and Mountain Madness team reach summit	29,028
	2:00–2:15 p.m	More climbers reach summit	
	3:00 p.m	Taiwanese team leader Gau reaches summit	
	3:30 p.m	Other climber reaches summit	
	3:40 p.m	Mountain Madness leader Fischer reaches summit	
	4:00 p.m	Adventure Consultant leader Rob Hall reaches summit just before client Doug Hansen	
⑥	5:00–5:20 p.m	Beildeman assumes leadership of groups along with Groom	27,600
⑦	4:40–6:00 p.m	Some team members return to Camp IV	25,900
⑧	5:00 p.m	First radio call from Hall requesting help	27,000
⑨	8:00 p.m	Group led by Beidleman becomes lost at South Col, just 300 yards from Camp IV	26,000
⑩	12:00 p.m	Group led by Beidleman finds way back to Camp IV and Boukreev retrieves remaining climbers	
⑪	**May 11** 10:00 a.m.	Rescue party finds Fischer and Gau but is only able to retrieve Gau	
⑫	4:30 p.m	Weathers returns to Camp IV unaided	
⑬	6:30 p.m.	Hall talks to wife final time	

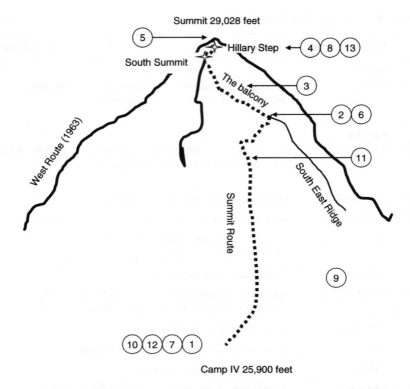

Figure I **Map of key events and locations as seen from the Southeast Ridge route**

during the final 72 hours. Figure 1 provides a visual presentation of events relative to their location on Everest summit.

Learning points

▶ On Mt Everest in May 1996, eight climbers from three expedition teams died. In total, 15 climbers died on the mountain in 1996, marking the worst death toll in Everest history. The same year, 98 climbers made successful summits and returned to safety.

▶ By ignoring pre-established turnaround times, the teams on Everest continued to pursue their goal of reaching the summit and ignored the potential consequences of such continued action.

▶ The history of climbing Everest and changes in the way climbing expeditions were organized may have set the stage for a changed relationship between leader and follower. The changing nature of climbing created a situation in which individual climbers relied more heavily on paid guides to help them to the top.

Learning questions

▶ Think of a time when you set and pursued a difficult or challenging goal. Be as specific as you can about the goal and what you did to pursue the goal. What sacrifices did you make to obtain the goal?

▶ How did you know when you achieved the goal? What was your measure of success?

▶ Did you set any timetable or any criteria for when you should abandon the goal? If not, did you abandon the goal or redefine what it meant to succeed at your goal at any time?

▶ What motivated you to pursue the goal?

2 "Why Haven't They Turned Around?": The Search for Answers

You think about achieving the goal almost constantly. Your training, diet, and waking hours are devoted to it. Some say you are obsessed, but you know now what it means to have a sense of purpose. You continue to direct more attention and resources to attaining the goal. Your family and friends, once excited about the idea of summiting Everest, have heard about its dangers. They have heard that about 1 in 6 do not make it back alive. You quickly remind them that reliable statistics are hard to come by in a country that does not keep formal records on the mountain.

By now, most of the people close to you support your goal to achieve the summit or at least know better than to question your goal in front of you. They support you through their silence. Some may plead for you to abandon your dream, but you know that is just not possible. You've already committed to successfully achieving the goal. You won't be turning back now, even though you haven't even left for the trip. Even though achieving the goal is far off, and many contingencies can sidetrack your success, you imagine what it must be like to summit Everest. It becomes your identity, and others too begin to see you as a successful climber. You are going for the big one, Everest, the legend. It's difficult to distinguish how you imagine your successful summit attempt from the actual pursuit itself. Your goal now becomes legitimate, and pursuing the summit becomes a goal unto itself. While others seek to explain your behavior, your passion for achieving the goal does not sway. But why have you become so focused on such a narrow goal?

While Chapter 1 described the pursuit and descent from the summit of Everest, Chapter 2 seeks reasons for the tragic results. By reviewing current thinking on leadership and teamwork, the chapter reviews several explanations for what occurred on Everest. In the end, the chapter suggests that, while each explanation sheds light on the Everest events, none is complete in and of itself.

Climber and soon-to-be rescue party member Ed Viesturs sat at camp anticipating his opportunity to summit. He looked through a telescope at a queue of climbers bottlenecked just below the summit of Mt Everest.

Viewing the traffic jam, he wondered why the leaders failed to direct their climber back down the mountain. Viesturs stood astonished that the climbers failed to abide by the pre-established turnaround times. Viesturs knew that the teams began to tread close to disaster by staying on the mountain so late into the afternoon. An even greater concern lied in the fact that the leaders themselves did not enforce the turnaround time. Viesturs posed the most central question of the events when he asked, *"They've already been climbing 14 hours, and they still aren't on the summit. Why haven't they turned around?"* (Coburn, 1997, p. 20).

A more general way to phrase his question might be, Why would a group continue to pursue a goal despite mounting evidence it could not be attained? Viesturs' question is important not just for climbers but for goal-setting and pursuit in any organization: for the manager who will engage in unethical behavior, risking one's career, just to gain advantages in one's sales figures; for the team of executives who pursue the company's short-term profits at the expense of its long-term survival; for the warrior, set on a particular course of action, who ignores shifts in the enemy's defensive strategies and continues with his original plan; for the company that holds tight to a once-successful business strategy, despite mounting evidence that the business environment has changed and the old strategy is no longer a success. Finding an answer to Viesturs' question of why the Everest teams continue to pursue the summit can inform our understanding of why leaders in a variety of organizations overpursue goals.

To find an explanation to Viesturs' question, we might turn to existing research on leadership, teams, and goal-setting. A rich and important body of knowledge exists and can inform the search for an answer. Three potential explanations for why teams overpursue goals arise time and time again: the leader's ambition and style, dysfunctional psychological processes, and the experience of leaders and followers.

Potential explanation 1: Ambition and style

One explanation for what occurred on Everest can be found in descriptions of how individual ambition drives leaders. The drive to achieve lofty heights and the ambition to make a unique contribution can lead individuals to put normal discretion aside. The ambition explanation looks at the psychological make-up of leaders and the groups they lead. This position holds that a better understanding of the team leader's disposition will shed light on what style of leader would continue for the summit and what style of person would turn around. This explanation suggests that those who would pursue the summit are extreme psychological types.

The ambition explanation served as the basis for one of the first systematic studies of climbing Everest in 1963, with the American Mt Everest Expedition (AMEE). The humanist psychologist James Lester was one of the first to see that the systemmatic study of Everest climbs could provide valuable insight into leadership and teamwork in general. Funded by the U.S. Navy, Lester and a crew of researchers gathered the 1963 AMEE team in Berkeley, California, and administered a battery of personality, stress, and psychological well-being tests (Lester, 1983).

Lester did not confine his study to the climbers' attitudes at sea level. A few months later, along with his fellow researchers, Lester traveled to the base of Mt Everest and climbed up the mountain to Camp II with the teams. The teams Lester studied included 17 American climbers, about 35 Sherpas, and hundreds of support staff. Writing a retrospective 20 years later, Lester described the team members as possessing

> considerable restlessness, dislike for routine, desire for autonomy, tendency to be dominant in personal relations, and a lack of interest in social interactions for its own sake. Their felt need for achievement and independence was very high. Given these characteristics, one can readily see how that which these men define as "stressful" might be different than what others identify with that term. (Lester, 1983, p. 34)

Later studies appear to confirm Lester's findings, at least in part. Studying a more culturally diverse group of Everest climbers than Lester's AMEE team, one researcher went to Everest base camp and started handing out personality surveys to climbers. Taking advantage of the downtime between training and acclimatization runs up the mountain, the researchers surveyed 39 climbers who spoke and read English but who were native to eight different countries (Eagan and Stelmack, 2003). The research shed additional light on the psychological make-up of elite Everest climbers. The study found that climbers, on average, displayed higher-than-normal results on two key personality dimensions:

1. *Extroversion*: Climbers liked to be around people and were energized by human interaction. The climbers were also disposed to higher risk taking and assertiveness.
2. *Achievement orientation*: The climbers were aggressive, dominant, and self-determined. This included a kind of tough-mindedness, determination, and resolve.

The climbers scored lower on only one characteristic:

▶ *Neuroticism*. The Everest sample showed a lower overall sense of worry and low reaction to stressful events. In other words, the climbers were less likely to panic.

This study seemed to suggest that Everest climbers were a socially engaged bunch of high achievers who maintained their calm under stress. But a survey of the 1985 Norwegian expedition showed a somewhat different profile (Breivik, 1996). The survey included seven of the eight Norwegian team members (unfortunately Chris Bonington, the best known of the bunch, was not measured). These climbers were compared with an additional 38 climbers. This second group also consisted of "elite" Norwegian climbers, but none in this second group had been to Everest. The study then compared these results with results from a group of English, Italian, and Czechoslovakian climbers who had participated in other studies.

Unlike the earlier studies of predominantly English-speaking climbers, this study found two distinct styles of climbers. Style 1 consisted of introverted, high-sensation-seeking, and highly anxious individuals, as demonstrated by the English and Italian expeditions. Style 2 consisted of a group of individuals who showed tough-mindedness, independence, and low anxiety and guilt, which was demonstrated by the Czech and Norwegian teams.

This study seems to confirm cultural differences between the styles of Everest climbers in general, although it is not clear if these cultural differences impact the climbers' decision-making. However, considering the styles or ambitions of climbers compared with the population as a whole and other elite climbers, Everest climbers were

▶ more driven to achieve
▶ unlikely to panic or become anxious during a crisis or problems
▶ less likely to view situations as "risky"
▶ more likely to take actions even when their decisions were viewed as risky.

An interesting insight emerges from these studies. While the Everest climbers do have some statistically extreme personality traits, especially compared with the average person, the climbers were more like the average individual than they were different. While climbers may be more driven, more likely to take on risk, and more likely to stay cool under pressure, Everest climbers seem "normal" on most other measures. Ambitious climbers were just as likely to abandon any one attempt at the summit and return another day.

In short, the ambition and style explanation fails to show why some goal-setting efforts drive success while others result in failure. Further, research has been unable to isolate if differences exist between climbers who have successfully achieved the summit and those who have not. Individual differences may account for those who engage in risky behavior, whether that behavior involves climbing a mountain or taking a financial risk, but differences in the ambition and style of climbers fail to distinguish between those who doggedly pursue a mountain summit and those who are likely to turn back safely. Nonetheless, as we will see later in the book, while individual difference does not hold the key to the question of group overpursuit of goals, it does provide insight into the process.

Potential explanation 2: Dysfunctional psychological process

A second explanation lies in the notion that groups develop dysfunctional psychological processes that lead to poor decision-making. The dysfunctional group psychology approaches focus on the irrational decision-making that emerges in group settings. The major conclusion of the dysfunctional group process camp lies in the idea that emotions take over rational thinking and lead to bad decisions.

A variety of these group explanations exist. Each relies on some hidden, if not unconscious, group psychological process that interferes with rational decision-making. The explanations include a variety of memorable titles. "Risky shift" describes how groups make riskier decisions on average than individuals (see Brown, 2000, pp. 199–212). "Groupthink" is the notion that groups form consensus too quickly and members of groups seek a kind of esprit de corps that limits critical thinking. "Abilene Paradox" suggests that teams prefer nonaction over the risk of failure— that individuals fear taking action, a form of so-called "action anxiety."

With groupthink, for example, the individuals in a team desire to belong. Because the individuals want to be seen as contributing group members, they will not criticize or challenge other group members. This desire for cohesion and esprit de corps and the fear of retaliation or rejection from others preclude questioning the group. The result is that members agree to a course of action too quickly. Groupthink provides a popular explanation for why groups make bad decisions and provides a potent explanation for the question of goal overpursuit (Janis, 1972).

Psychological explanations such as groupthink have experienced wide acceptance because they resonate with people's experience in a variety of settings. For example, Jerry Harvey, formerly a professor at George Washington University, describes how Abilene Paradox emerges in the context of corporate research and development projects where companies will not abandon pie-in-the-sky ideas, even after they prove elusive. Harvey describes the phenomenon in the context of interpersonal relationships, a couple who goes to the altar because of what could happen if the wedding were abandoned. Psychological dysfunction provides a convincing way to show how what should be is eclipsed by irrational desires (Harvey, 1996).

Indeed, these concepts provide handy and actionable means to notice and correct dysfunctional team behavior and leadership gone awry. However, each of these theories fails to explain what happened on Everest. Years of research show that groups are just as likely to make more conservative decisions as risky ones. On Everest, a number of teams abandoned their summit attempts, and individual members of other teams decided to turn around at reasonable times. This discounts the theory of risky shift. The Everest teams showed little evidence of esprit de corps or cohesion, essential for groupthink to be an explanation. Finally, the teams did anything but fear action. In fact, the teams took action, continuing to the summit, even when the action should have been feared. In the end, the explanations that rely primarily on dysfunctional group process fail to provide a compelling or complete explanation for what happened on Everest.

Potential explanation 3: Past experience

A third line of thinking also deserves attention as a means to explain what happened on Everest. This line of thinking focuses on a leader's prior experience and past performance. This perspective suggests that when individuals rely too much on past experience, they inevitably get into trouble because past experience often falls short in the face of new and changing events. Typically, this line of thinking points to either past failure or past success as an indicator of future action. This perspective could be applied to Everest. The team leaders that had successfully summited in the past would be likely to use the same strategies for getting to the top again. In contrast, those leaders that had failed in the past would likely try different strategies to get to the top. This perspective seems to offer a compelling explanation for what occurred on Everest, but it too lacks the power to explain all that occurred.

One study showed just how difficult it is for leaders to rely on past experience as an indicator of success, even when past experience proved successful. A group of researchers looked at how companies in two U.S. transportation industries responded to deregulation. They looked at the US airline industry, which was deregulated in 1978 by the Civil Aviation

Board, and the trucking industry, which was deregulated by the Motor Carrier Act of 1980 (Audia, Locke, and Smith, 2000).

The research focused on organizational strategies before and after deregulation. For example, before deregulation, companies in the trucking industry focused mainly on the quality of services provided and the transportation of specialized goods as ways to differentiate one company from another. After deregulation, some trucking companies focused on containing labor costs by using independent drivers. Another strategy used by trucking companies after deregulation was to concentrate business in certain high-use areas of the country, thus concentrating their expenses on a few, highly profitable routes. In the airline industry, before deregulation, strategies focused on adding flights to existing routes or focusing on quality. After deregulation, companies focused on connecting flights using a "hub" system, being a low-cost provider, or catering to deep-pocket business travelers.

The study found that companies that performed better the 5 years prior to deregulation were more likely to maintain their current strategies. Companies with poorer performance before deregulation were more likely to develop new strategies after deregulation rather than maintain the same strategies. Ultimately, the study found that transportation companies could not rely on prior success or prior failure to determine what course of action to take in the future.

The finding, coupled with a number of other studies that sought to determine if past success and failures could determine action, revealed that prior *success* in achieving goals may be dysfunctional because success builds unfounded confidence in existing strategies. At the same time, prior *failure* in achieving goals may be dysfunctional because it threatens the self-identity of the individual. Taken as a whole, this research suggests that neither past success nor past failure to achieve goals seems to be a good indicator of success when conditions change. Taking actions based on past achievements or actions will inevitably lead to failure if the environment is different. Success leads to overconfidence, and failure leads to threats to the ego. In the final analysis, while past experience provides some insight to the question of continued goal pursuit, it fails to provide a conclusive answer.

Need for a more complete answer

Leadership theories and research fail to provide a complete explanation for the tragedy because they do not account for the potentially dysfunctional aspects of goals and goal-setting. Each position presented above offered a partial explanation. The ambition of leaders and followers to achieve a goal drove them to the summit but failed to explain why these very same climbers had turned around in similar situations in the past. The dysfunctional group theory failed to explain why the groups displayed both positive and negative signs of effective group processes. Finally, the past experience explanation failed to differentiate between past failures and past successes and how they impacted the present situation.

In study after study, research comes to one conclusion. In most cases, goals provide motivation to pursue greater and more ambitious achievements. Goals increase effort toward achieving specific outcomes; that is true. But in just as many cases, putting in more effort to the same course of action results in ultimate failure. Something in the goal-setting and goal-pursuit process itself must have been involved.

Any explanation of the Everest disaster requires serious consideration of how the leaders and their teams set and pursued their goal of achieving the summit. An adequate explanation of what happened on Everest needs to examine how the teams described and justified the process of goal pursuit. Analysis of the events consistently revealed how leaders and their followers came to identify with future as yet unachieved goals. At times, it seemed that achieving the goal became the leader's primary source of identity.

Goal striving in the 1963 American Expedition

The role of goals in forming and maintaining an identity can be highlighted by an observation made concerning the 1963 AMEE. A group of researchers followed the summit teams from February 20 to May 22 (Emerson, 1966). In addition to observing team members, researchers requested that climbers fill out a daily diary of thoughts and experiences. Researchers were particularly interested in the role that goals played in sustaining climbers' efforts to reach the summit. Researchers concluded that the more uncertainty the climbers faced, the more likely they were to sustain effort at reaching the summit. In other words, as confidence in reaching the summit decreased, efforts increased.

The AMEE provided a unique opportunity to study differences in team goal striving because two different summit teams developed within the expedition. Each summit team chose a different strategy to reach the summit. One team, called the South Col team, focused on reaching the summit via the South Col route. The South Col route had already proven successful in prior expeditions. During the trek to base camp, however, interest in an alternative route began to take hold among a subgroup of climbers. This subgroup favored the never-attempted route along the Western Ridge of Everest.

The researchers asked members of each of the two summit teams to record their degree of pessimism or optimism in achieving the summit by either the Western Ridge or the South Col routes. Over time, the Western Ridge team grew more pessimistic of their likelihood of achieving success while the South Col team stayed about the same in their confidence of reaching the summit through the established route. It seemed that there was growing pessimism among both subteams that the untried western route could lead to success.

What the researchers did next was even more interesting. They looked to see what kinds of information each team was using to make judgments about pessimism or optimism. They found some startling information. First, they found that the more uncertain climbers felt about their possible success in reaching the summit, the more likely they were to invest in their particular strategy. Uncertainty increased commitment to the goal. Second, certain learning patterns emerged that reinforced the uncertainty. Two interesting patterns emerged. First, each team sought information that challenged what prevailed in the environment. For example, if a weather report suggested a clear sky, the group might seek information to indicate the sky may actually be cloudy. The second pattern of learning involved a high degree of negative feedback. In other words, the teams sought information that confirmed they were not making any progress or would encounter unforeseen obstacles. The researchers concluded that goal pursuit emerged as a self-referential loop. The more the team strived for the goal, the more the team sought information that increased uncertainty about achieving the goal. The increased uncertainty led the teams to invest more energy into achieving the goal.

The study conducted on the 1963 AMEE provides some of the first evidence of goal-striving on Mt Everest, as the researchers concluded that goal-striving is a self-maintaining system (Emerson, 1966, p. 227). It was first exposed that the Everest teams sought to reinforce existing beliefs. Ultimately, it did not matter if the teams were uncertain about obtaining the summit. The teams learned what they wanted to learn in order to maintain their goal.

Close identification with the future goal of reaching the summit serves a useful purpose: it appeals to followers with a vision of a desired future. Without the goal the purpose of being a team failed to exist. In fact, the language of goals assumes an almost religious status in many organizations because goals serve an important social function. Goals forge a shared identity among group members. Goals catalyze a common direction. Goals help leaders gain the support of weary followers. Goals commonly become the very identity of the group. This process, while often beneficial to leaders and comforting to followers, can go too far, as when a group looks to the goal for its sole source of identity. When both leaders and followers begin to identify too closely with the future goal, the normally functional process of goal-setting begins to go astray.

Keep in mind that not all goal-directed behavior results in negative consequences. In many circumstances, the opposite is true: the pursuit of goals leads to success. The advantages of goal-setting get lost, however, because psychological, social, and contextual factors make abandoning the goal unthinkable once the goal-setting process begins. Justifying the pursuit of goals becomes more important than achieving the goal. A look at mountain climbers and other goal-pursuing enthusiasts brings a view of goal-setting as a process that can go off track. In the Everest events as in other stories, goal-setting often carried unintended consequences. At times, it seemed that achieving the goal became the leader's and climbers' primary source of social identity.

As Everest survivor Beck Weathers conceded, the events on Everest may be about the overpursuit of goals. He speculated in an emotional interview after the events, "You can overpursue goals. You can become obsessed with goals." Weathers, like the studies reviewed here, exposed the fact that goal-setting, despite its many benefits, has a troubling side. Goals become difficult to abandon, provide a handy language to justify undesirable action, lead to unintended consequences, and under some conditions lead to unethical behavior. The Everest teams represent one of the most compelling examples of how goal-setting can lead organizations down the wrong path under certain conditions. The overwhelming desire to ascend the summit allowed the teams to justify risky behavior and idealize their situation beyond what was reasonable. The goal of reaching the summit of Everest led to its destructive pursuit, the process of *goalodicy*.

Learning points

▶ This chapter posed the question: Why would a group continue to pursue a goal despite mounting evidence it could not be obtained? Three explanations were put forth:

1. The ambition and style of the leader and climbers
2. Dysfunctional leadership and group psychological processes
3. The prior experience of the team.

▶ Each explanation is inadequate in and of itself because each failed to account for the nature of goals and the goal-setting process.
▶ Destructive goal pursuit is at the heart of the explanation to the Everest disaster.

Learning questions

▶ Why do you think so little attention has been paid to the negative consequences of goals?
▶ Think back to Chapter 1 and your individual goals. How difficult would it have been to abandon your goal once you began pursuing it? What factors would have kept you from abandoning your goal? What factors would have allowed you to abandon your goal?
▶ Thinking back on your own individual goals, what unintended consequences emerged from pursuing and possibly achieving the goal?

Part II Destructive Goal Pursuit

3 The Problem of Goalodicy: The Unintended Consequences of Goal Pursuit

Pursuing the summit of Everest becomes part of who you are. Your self-image becomes inseparable from the summit. Contingencies, unintended consequences, and other obstacles attempt to get in your way but ultimately fail to distract you. And distractions they are, since such obstacles only remind you to focus on what is important—achieving your goal. You focus on the summit. You become determined to meet your goal. The goal itself is straightforward: summit the mountain. You know, at least in theory, how this can be done. You put trust in the expedition leaders, and they reassure you that they have it all figured out. Stay the course, don't get distracted, and listen to their guidance. Don't worry about the inevitable setbacks, such as the lack of sleep, the uncomfortable cough, the egos of your climbing partners. Focus on attaining your goal. You don't need to worry about finding excuses because you will have success. Your sense of self and the goal have become inseparable.

This chapter introduces the term *goalodicy* as a way to understand destructive goal pursuit and identifies the limits of goals. Goalodicy, the idea that goals and the goal-setting process can stifle progress, remains difficult to believe. As with the corporation that engages in extensive strategic planning and implementation efforts only to see its stock price fall or the company that sets out to increase revenue only to see its sales decrease, the disappointments that emerge are painful not just because of their toll on self-esteem but also because the energy invested extracts the very opposite of what the company set out to achieve. On Everest, goalodicy set in as leaders and their teams continued to pursue the distant summit, ignoring signs that many of the climbers should have abandoned the goal. Putting goalodicy into context, however, begins not with Everest, but with a trip back about 2000 years to the classic stories told by Greeks and Romans.

Perspectives from mythology

In the epic story *The Georgics*, the poet Virgil alludes to the story of Leander and his love, the beautiful Hero. Each evening Hero would hang a lamp outside her window to beacon Leander for a visit. The lantern beckoned Leander to swim across the sea that separates Asia from Europe to visit his lovely Hero. Guided singularly by the dim light, Leander swam across the channel each night without incident. One night as the winter brought violent waters, Leander and Hero agreed to postpone their courtship. But Leander, in his great desire for Hero, failed to heed an oncoming storm. The heavy storm blew out the light, unbeknownst to Hero, who waited patiently for her Leander to arrive. Without the dim light to guide his way, Leander had no knowledge of which direction to swim for safety. Leander became lost in the water, "swimming in the black of night . . . above him thunders the vast gate of heaven" (Virgil, 1982). Leander became stranded and caught in the waves. In the end, Leander died in pursuit of his love.

Leander relied on a distant image to guide his way. Similarly, leaders and their followers may find themselves trapped when committed to a distant goal that suddenly becomes snuffed in the night. Without the goal, the teams may find themselves with no direction. The events of Everest provide a vivid example of groups who, committed to a distant goal, may fall into disarray when the future goal suddenly and irreversibly vanishes in the night. One can imagine Leander taking undue risk, overly committed to the prospect of his nightly journey, swimming into the oncoming storm and being lured by the beauty of Hero.

The story of Leander and Hero illustrates how men and women can be lured by a distant light, how they will risk everything to accomplish a goal. This theme, that goals often blind individuals to the risks they face, appeared often in Greek and Roman stories. Sophocles, the Greek poet, writing nearly 400 years before Virgil, quipped in *Fragments*, "Every person can see things far off but is blind to what is near." Sophocles points us to a kind of farsightedness that often accompanies goal-setting. This farsightedness means that it is easier to imagine a far-off destination than it is to recognize the challenges and difficulties faced in the present.

Sophocles may have had Ate in mind when he quipped about farsightedness. Ate, a daughter of Zeus, was known as the temptress. Ate knew people's hidden desires and tempted them to take unnecessary risks in order to fulfill those desires. Ate was likely there, tempting Leander to risk it all to reach Hero.

Ate was also likely there challenging sailors to endure the hardships of sea to reach the far-off destination of Ithaca, as recounted in the more contemporary poem by Constantinos Cavafy. Ate was probably the one telling weary sailors to forget about their fears, boredom, and loneliness by envisioning the port of Ithaca, a real yet fantastical island. For the sailors, Ithaca represents the goal of their trip, the justification for their troubles. The destination justifies the goal.

Ate was there tempting the climbers on Everest to take undue risk to accomplish their dreams. Such utopias, like goals themselves, offer the security of a narrowly focused vision of the future. These visions remain unclouded by the complexities and realities that will be encountered during their pursuit.

Regardless of the setting or the time frame, the same mechanisms of farsightedness contribute to destructive goal pursuit. This farsightedness may help explain the disaster on Mt Everest. The goal of reaching the summit promised an idealistic, far-off utopia, worth striving for, but blinding the climbers, literally and figuratively, to the difficult realities of the present.

The problem of goalodicy

Farsightedness comes with the often-unrecognized and little-understood situation in which goal-setting carries negative consequences. To highlight that the negative consequences of goal-setting have begun to set in, the terms *goal* and *theodicy* were combined to form the term *goalodicy*. The "goal" part of this word highlights the future-oriented quality of goalodicy, so that a goal can be seen as an idealized future state, an optimal outcome. The "theodicy" part of this word emphasizes that current information is ignored for fear that it means that the goal will not be achieved. Goalodicy is a useful notion to show that some or all of the negative consequences of goals have begun to set in.

Philosophers use the term *theodicy* to describe how people who hold strong beliefs often seek to maintain that belief, even in the face of contradictory information. The problem of theodicy has been nettlesome for philosophers for as long as bad things have happened to good people. Theodicies offer explanations when current beliefs about the nature of the world are challenged by seemingly inexplicable events. The German sociologist Max Weber (1964) described theodicy as the situation when individuals rely on future desired states to rationalize current suffering. Problems such as how evil can exist in a just world or how innocent people can experience hardship might be answered by statements such as "Innocent people suffer because they perpetuated evil in a prior life" or "Evil will be eradicated and evil people will be punished in the future" (Berger, 1967, p. 58).

Taken together, a goal theodicy, or goalodicy, describes how the individual, team, or group fails to abandon a goal, thus allowing for destructive goal pursuit to set in. In addition, goalodicy implies that the goal itself allows individuals to rationalize such behavior. Like the theodicy talked about by philosophers, goalodicy implies that individuals use the future as yet unachieved goal to rationalize the continued pursuit of the goal. The goal serves not only as the destination, but also as the means to justify the continued pursuit of the goal.

Goalodicy can be summarized as follows: the more a person, group, or organization relies on a future as yet unachieved goal as a source of identity, the more likely they will persist at pursuing the goal beyond what is reasonable. The goal setter or setters will continue to invest more resources in achieving the goal, which increases the likelihood that achieving the goal will result in unforeseen and often detrimental outcomes. The goal setter may even risk his or her own demise to reach the goal. Ultimately, the goal becomes the primary identity of the goal setter, and abandoning the goal becomes as unthinkable as abandoning oneself (Kayes, 2005, p. 393).

Goalodicy emerges as leaders and their followers begin to ignore new information, especially when this information contradicts current beliefs about achieving the goal. Goalodicy provides a tool to maintain the motivating power of goals, even when new information may indicate that the goal cannot be achieved. The problem of goalodicy lies in the following complication. Goals motivate leaders and their followers to continue to put more effort into achieving a desired outcome. In many cases, however, the additional effort will not lead to goal achievement. Goalodicy describes a situation in which the more effort that is put into achieving the goal, the more likely the goal will be destructive.

Goalodicy emerges from the complex interaction of a variety of psychological, social, and environmental processes. When this complex mix of factors comes together, the normally helpful process of goal-setting and pursuit becomes dysfunctional.

Consequences of goalodicy on Everest

The pursuit of the summit in 1996 provides an example of the consequences of goalodicy. First, as the teams pushed for the summit, pursuing their goal with unparalleled effort, they found it nearly impossible to abandon their goal. As the teams became more and more driven by the attainment of the goal, they identified more and more with the distant as yet unachieved goal. Second, new and contradictory information continued to suggest the goal could not be safely attained, yet many of the leaders and team members chose to ignore these signs. The teams failed to learn from this information that ultimately could have saved all their lives. Third, the leaders also took unnecessary risks by pushing weaker climbers to the summit when they should have turned back. Fourth and finally, the actions of the leaders led to putting some followers' interests over those of others, a situation some have considered ethically questionable.

The limits of goals

Goalodicy offers a warning for those wishing to pursue ambitious goals, like the summit of Everest. Goalodicy reminds us that ambitious people may seek to accomplish seemingly insurmountable goals by pushing themselves and their communities to the limits, only to encounter the limits of their own capacity. But while the stories share the same quality of human dilemma, the ancients lived in very different times. Much of the analysis of Greek tragedy, like the story of Leander, focuses on how hubris, or ego, emerges from human limitation (Elmes and Barry, 1999). Everest reveals a different type of human dilemma: the limits of goals and the goal-setting process. The events illustrate how goals can lull leaders and those around them into complacency and narrow thinking.

Greek and Roman literature ground the present conversation about leadership and goals. The Greeks too believed in the future as much as in the past. The Western tradition of storytelling remains replete with stories of how solutions can be found in the future resolution of a dilemma, if we just stay our course. There is no need to worry about the present; future solutions will emerge to put us at ease.

Like Ate, tempting with the promise of success, goals tempted the climbers on Everest into a pattern of climbing that blinded them to the complications that began to emerge: ailing climbers, increased complexity, growing lateness of the hour, and the impending storm. The Greeks and Romans provide us with stories of ill-fated attempts at goal-setting, but more contemporary and systematic research also confirms some of the limits of goals. Research notes at least four limitations of goals and the goal-setting process.

GOALS ARE DIFFICULT TO ABANDON

Psychologists have shown how gamblers, investors, and other high-stakes goal setters continue to throw good money at bad goals. Research confirms that many people find it difficult to change direction once a particular course is established. Psychologist Barry Staw has spent decades studying how individuals, groups, and organizations continue to "throw good money after bad" by continuing to invest resources in a failing course of action. For example, Ross and Staw (1993) conducted an analysis of Long Island Lighting Company's decision to build a nuclear power plant in the northeastern United States. At first, financial analysts projected the cost of building the Shoreham plant at about $75 million, a relatively acceptable cost by 1966 standards. However, over the ensuing 23 years, costs spiraled out of control. Despite the growing costs, the power company continued to invest more and more money into the project. In the end, over $5 billion was spent on a project that never generated a single kilowatt of electricity. Investors finally abandoned the project. As Staw notes, "One analyst described [the behavior of the utility] as 'sort of like a heroin addict,' adding 'You have to keep pumping in money' " (Ross and Staw, 1993, p. 711).

Although Staw and colleagues point to mechanisms other than goals per se to explain why individuals failed to abandon the project, the implications for goal-setting become clear. Once an organization establishes a goal, it tends to continue in the same direction rather than adjust course, even when the course of action leads to failure. This may be why Staw calls this phenomenon "escalation of commitment to a failing course of action." Just as escalation of commitment results from prior failing action, prior success can also lead to failure.

According to the researchers who studied changes in the transportation industry, as mentioned in Chapter 2 successful goal achievement may result from two factors. The first is power relations in groups and how groups that hold beliefs about successful strategies maintain power. This first factor suggests that leadership, as far as it relates to power, provides an important lens to understand why organizations engage in the destructive pursuit of goals. Second, leaders require specific skills to learn in the face of change. These two factors are important because they suggest mechanisms to overcome destructive goal pursuit.

The power relations among group members and the specific skills of the leader probably played roles in the Everest incident, as will be discussed in later chapters. The Everest debacle provides further evidence that abandoning goals become difficult once a course of action has begun. By focusing attention on a distant, often idealized, future goal, goals inspire action directed toward the goal, not to potential changes in the environment. The inspiration of *what goal* can be achieved, rather than the difficulties of *how* to achieve that goal, diverts attention from the resources, sacrifices, and consequences that will result when pursuing the goal. As Everest demonstrates, goals become difficult to abandon once a compelling direction for their pursuit has begun.

GOALS LIMIT LEARNING

Even well-intentioned goals carry unintended consequences. Goals may be achieved at the expense of learning. One of the most important yet troubling findings from research is that goals may actually decrease effectiveness in the face of complex tasks. Researchers asked participants to determine future stock prices for 100 imaginary firms. Researchers provided only a limited amount of information about the firms to each of the participants. This left much about the firms unknown so that the participants had to make decisions with a limited amount of information. Researchers then assigned the participants to one of two groups. The researchers told the first group to meet a specific difficult goal: to guess the stock price within $10 of the actual stock price. In contrast, researchers told the second group to "do your best." The researchers knew that estimating the stock prices correctly would be a difficult task since in pre-tests individuals estimated the stock price correctly only about 15 percent of the time (Earley, Connolly, and Ekegren, 1989).

What the researchers discovered turned conventional wisdom on goal-setting on its head. Participants who had high and specific goals were less successful than those who were simply told to do their best. This finding baffled researchers since study after study had shown that "do your best" goals were less successful than setting specific measurable goals. In fact, according to some observers, the view that specific goals improved performance over "do your best" goals was one of the most influential findings in all of the research on management and leadership. The researchers were so baffled by their findings that they reran the experiment three more times. In each experiment, groups that were told to do their best in estimating stock prices outperformed groups with specific goals.

The researchers also found that the group with specific goals tried more and different strategies in an attempt to achieve their goal. The fact that this tactic was not successful seemed counterintuitive. Would not trying out different strategies mean that the participants were more likely to learn the best strategy? In many cases, that might be true. However, this task proved different. The researchers intentionally designed the task so that several different strategies might produce correct or near-correct responses. The possibilities were so numerous, in fact, that trying different strategies became counterproductive. There were just too many possible strategies that could prove effective that the participants could not realistically learn the strategy that worked through normal trial and error.

The research revealed an important but little talked about dimension of goal-setting. Goal-setting works best when effort, not learning, is paramount. Setting and pursuing challenging goals is a good strategy to follow when you want to increase the effort that people put forth to accomplish a goal. In some cases, however, like the stock-predicting strategy just described, where learning is paramount, goal-setting actually has a negative effect on reaching the goal. Too much effort actually got in the way of making good decisions. The researchers concluded that when a task can be achieved by many possible solutions, then goal-setting actually limits effectiveness. They concluded that goal-setting is better suited to solutions where quantity rather than quality of output is best. In the face of novel and complex tasks, simply trying your best may be more effective than trying to reach a specific goal.

GOALS INCREASE RISK TAKING

Another unintended consequence of setting and pursuing challenging goals is that goals themselves may encourage unduly risky behavior. That was the finding of a study conducted by a group of goal-setting advocates. The research team studied a group of students playing video games. The researchers observed that the participants were more likely to engage in risky behavior when they had difficult performance goals. Researchers drew the conclusion that higher goals may encourage riskier behavior (Knight, Durham, and Locke, 2001).

The finding that goals may produce riskier behavior is important. It implies that goals allow leaders to take chances, justify risks, and avoid normal accountability. On Everest, leaders at all levels overlooked obvious problems. The goal of reaching the summit became so ingrained in the identities of the group that the leaders could easily justify violating pre-established turnaround times. Goal-setting remains an essential part of organizational success, but overly risky behavior that results from goals can lead to all kinds of problems in organizations, including unethical behavior.

PURSUIT OF GOALS MAY LEAD TO UNETHICAL BEHAVIOR

Growing evidence in controlled laboratory experiments supports another claim against goals that may be the most troubling of all. Under some circumstances, stringent and demanding goals may encourage unethical behavior. A group of researchers asked a group of participants to create as many words as possible from a list of seven letters. This experiment, called an anagram, is a popular tool used by psychologists to test different aspects of task performance. The anagram task is simple and easy to understand.

The researchers created three groups and allowed each group to practice so that all participants had equal knowledge of how to perform the task.

It turned out that seven anagrams could be created in the allowed time frame. With the knowledge that the creation of seven anagrams was a reasonable performance standard, the researchers gave slightly different instructions to each of the groups. Researchers told the first group to "do your best" and then gave $10 to each person for participating. The researchers gave the second group an exact goal to "create nine words" from each anagram and gave each participant a flat $10 for participation. The researchers also gave the third group the goal of creating nine words but rewarded each participant with $2 for each time they met the goal.

The researchers found that two groups were more likely to overstate actual performance: those with reward-based goals, in the form of small financial incentives (Group 3), and those with clearly stated specific goals (Group 2). Individuals simply told to "do their best" were less likely to exaggerate performance. In addition, those that were closest to achieving their goals were more likely to overstate performance than those far from achieving their goals. In all, about 30 percent of participants with reward-based goals overstated their performance (Schweitzer, Ordonez, and Douma, 2004). The conclusion reached is that goals can actually encourage unethical behavior.

Students playing video games, playing the stock market and word games reveal some of the limitations and problems with goals. This chapter has outlined the dysfunctional aspects of goal-setting. The view of goal-setting put forth here is difficult to accept because it challenges some long-held beliefs about the positive value of goal-setting. The chapter has shown how goal-setting on Everest may have been one of the factors that led to disaster. The concept of goalodicy can be used as a way to describe these dysfunctions. The process of goalodicy is explored in more detail in the following chapters that look more specifically at how leadership and teamwork may play a part in the onset of goalodicy and lead teams, like those on Everest, into destructive goal pursuit.

Learning points

▶ Evidence of destructive goal pursuit can be seen in stories dating back at least since ancient Greece.
▶ *Goalodicy* is a term used to describe destructive goal pursuit. Goalodicy provides an alternative explanation of what occurred on Everest based on the dysfunctional pursuit of goals. Goalodicy works by allowing

teams to put off the reality of the present in hopes that achieving a
future goal will eliminate current obstacles.
▶ At least four limitations to goals exist:

1. Goals are difficult to abandon or change once set.
2. Goal limit learning and thus performance during complex tasks.
3. Goals increase risk taking.
4. Goals may lead to unethical behavior.

Learning questions

▶ How was goalodicy at play on Everest? What evidence was there that
goalodicy had taken hold of the Everest teams?
▶ How did the guides or team leaders encourage goalodicy?
▶ Can you think of other examples of goalodicy beyond what occurred
on Everest? What about examples from your own experience?

4 The Problem with Leadership: How Leadership Contributed to the Tragedy

You arrive at Katmandu in the Kingdom of Nepal—one of the most bizarre and underdeveloped cities in the world. The kingdom has only been open to westerners since the 1950s. You discover that modernity has only begun to trickle in. As your plane lands at the airport, you are shocked to see abandoned fuselages and old airplane engine parts littered just off the runway. You quickly become aware that you are in a place that has a different set of beliefs and habits.

After ensuring that your gear followed you to your destination, you collect your bags and head out of the terminal. You are immediately confronted with the sense of a country where the average annual income is about $300. The pollution invades your lungs. The mixture of two-stroke engine fuel, lead from unrefined gasoline, and dust from the dirt roads conspires in your lungs. As your chartered van pulls away, you are astounded to see what resembles a golf course overlooking a short hill as you make your way through to the city center.

You check into your prepaid hotel room and retreat from the heat of the day into the lush courtyard. The thick and heavy wall surrounding the hotel is reminiscent of a kind of long-lost imperialism. Young Nepalese waiters bring you a cool yogurt drink, and you hide from the sun under one of the canvas umbrellas placed strategically on the courtyard lawn. Breathing is difficult, even on your first day, but after a few days in the mile-high Katmandu your body will return to its normal breathing rate of about 12 times per minute.

In the garden, you are greeted by members of your expedition, and people begin exchanging stories. The stories reinforce everyone's identity as climbers, reassures everyone as to competence, and serves as a kind of psychological posturing. Everyone talks about their climbing experience. Many have tried and failed at Everest before; others are seeking the seven summits. Each person has a goal.

One thing for sure, the air on the first days set the tone for the rest of the trip. The tone is one of competition more than cooperation. You know from prior climbs that highly successful people are just as likely to form a great team as a bad team. The competition you feel with other team members could lead to a productive and sustained effort to the summit. In other teams, such an extensive offering of ambition has led to effective teamwork. But the feeling doesn't emerge this time. Instead, the differences between members lead everyone to feel marginalized. At the end of the first meeting, no one feels a part of the team.

The posturing that occurred at this first meeting doesn't give way. You don't feel like part of a group with a common identity. You begin to feel a dilemma. On the one hand, you identify closely with the mountain-climbing community; on the other hand, you feel alienated from your immediate team. You share an idealized goal but not the impeding reality.

Feeling alienated from your team, you begin to identify with your leader. Why wouldn't you? The leader's command of the situation at hand creates confidence. He tells stories of his successful summits. The leader's optimism is contagious and only fuels your summit fever. His personality engages at every turn. He tells stories where the outcomes seem unreal, like saving lives of stranded climbers and his own subsequent moves to save himself. If you once doubted your ability to belong to this group or questioned whether you could be a part of this team, the leader reassures you that you made the right decision to pursue your dream. The brotherhood and sisterhood of the rope may be a fragile alliance, but it provides the means to get you to the top of the mountain.

This chapter looks at the problem of leadership as it relates to goal pursuit. With all the studies, theories, and advocates of leadership, to pose leadership as a problem seems troublesome. This chapter focuses on the often-ignored limitations of depending on leadership when pursuing goals. Two limitations of leadership become evident in reviewing Everest. The first limitation rests in the problem of team member dependence on a leader. When team members become dependent on a leader to guide action, team members become stifled in their ability to learn. Because they are unable to learn, they become vulnerable to the vicissitudes of circumstance. The second limitation of leadership involves the limits of the leader. Leaders themselves experience limits in their ability to manage the complexity of a situation. In a complex and changing environment, no one individual holds the key to success, regardless of their capability.

In the final analysis, these limitations of leadership in the case of Everest, dependence and complexity, reveal a paradox inherent in team leadership. The relationship between Rob Hall and Beck Weathers provides a good place to explore this paradox. Unable to continue his ascent because of impaired vision, Weathers made a pact with his team leader, Hall. Weather would wait for the guide to return from the summit before beginning his descent. Hall directed Weathers not to descend for any reason before he returned. In a disquieting assurance to Hall, Weathers agreed to wait, "cross my heart and hope to die." In the ensuing hours, Weathers waited in the chilling cold as his body slowly lost its ability to keep warm. Weathers had at least two opportunities to descend with other climbers but refused to descend because of his pact with Hall. Finally, nearly 10 hours later, out of supplementary oxygen, sick from altitude, shivering in the cold, and nearly blind, Weathers agreed to descend with assistant guide Groom, who was in radio contact with Hall. What is chilling about this incident is that Weathers continued to wait for the leader despite his deteriorating condition. Only after all options became exhausted and he faced standing alone on the mountain did Weathers make a decision without Hall by joining the remaining group on its descent.

Weathers risked his own life to wait for Hall. Weathers' decision to wait for Hall points to two unsettling points about leadership. The first point is that Weathers became so dependent on the team leader and was virtually incapable of taking an action without direction from the leader. Second, Hall became faced with a nearly impossible situation: no matter what his choice, he would inevitably fail in one of his duties as a leader. Hall struggled to meet the obligation of helping both his ailing climbers and those continuing on the climb. These two limitations of leadership— the fact that leaders face competing, often irreconcilable, demands and the dysfunctional dependence of teams on leaders—serve as the basis for this chapter.

The circumstances faced independently by guides Fischer and Hall on Everest were similar in many key ways. For example, one of Hall's final actions on the mountain was helping his client Doug Hansen, who had collapsed near the summit and was unable to descend unaided. Hall may have felt a particular obligation to Hansen based on their past work together. The prior year, Hall had forced Hansen to turn around just a few hundred feet shy of the summit because he feared that Hansen would not be able to get down safely. Hall had encouraged Hansen to try again. It was rumored that Hall gave Hansen a deep discount in 1996 to encourage his participation in one last push for the summit. Hall had blamed Hansen's inability to reach the summit the prior year on the fact that ropes had not been fixed on the way up and that slowed Hansen and his team down.

Fischer may have been in a similar situation. Fischer's last action as a leader seems to have involved helping down the Taiwanese climber Gau. The final Sherpa rescue attempt found Fischer and Gau roped together on their descent. Unlike Hall and Hansen, however, Gau was not a client of Fischer; the two were not even on the same team. Some might have even suspected that Gau, as the leader of the Taiwanese team, looked more like a rival than a teammate. There is some debate, and Gau has contested the issue that Fischer was helping him down. Nonetheless, Fischer's history as a climber and leader suggests that he was able and ready to assist other climbers when they were in trouble (Bromet, 2005). Fischer risked his own life a few years earlier on the summit of K2 in his heroic efforts to save weak climbers and just days before the final push to the summit had helped an ailing climber.

The actions of Fischer and Hall remain so compelling because they exemplify the actions of a heroic and dependable leader. These are desirable attributes for leaders. While they say a lot about the leader personally, they say little about how the leader develops these or other important qualities among the team members. This is important to consider, because it is the team and its members, not just the leader, who must accomplish the goal.

Dysfunctional dependence

The failure of leaders to further develop team members limited the team members' abilities to make independent and thoughtful decisions. Lacking self-reliance, the teams became stifled, unable to respond to the problems at hand. More precisely, the members of the team, including the assistant guides, like Beidleman and Boukreev, became dependent on the leaders to make sense of and manage an increasingly challenging situation. While the team leaders established their authority and competence with team members, they failed to develop their team members' skills and abilities. The leader became established as the main decision maker on the team. When the leader became severed from the team, then the team members became unable to deal with the increasing complexity of the circumstances they faced.

The actions of leaders helped create this situation of authority and dependence on Everest. For example, the ABC television news magazine *Turning Point* pieced together a documentary in the aftermath of the disaster. In one short clip, leaders Hall, Fischer, and others huddled in a tent at base camp, planning for the final ascent. We hear Hall taking near sole responsibility for declaring and enforcing the summit turnaround schedule. He asserts his authority and its consequences. When enforcing turnaround times, Hall asserted, "I'll get unpopular, but somebody has to be unpopular sometimes" (ABC News, 1996b) or, "I will not tolerate dissention up there. My word will be absolute law, beyond appeal. If you don't like a particular decision I make, I'd be happy to discuss it with you afterward, but not while we're up on the hill" (from Krakauer, cited in Roberto and Carioggia, 2003).

Krakauer recounts Hall's absolute insistence that he enforce the turn-around times.

> [Hall] said, "I'm going to call the shots on summit day. If I say we turn around, we're going to turn around. Some of you are going to argue with me, you're not going to like it, but believe me, I know it's right." (ABC News, 1996b, p. 4)

Statements like these set the tone for dependence on the leader to enforce the turnaround time on summit day.

GROUP DEPENDENCE: A BRIEF HISTORY

Taken together, the actions and words of those on Everest serve as important examples of how leaders can build dysfunctional dependence in teams. To better understand how dysfunctional dependence emerges in a team and the role of the team leader in cultivating this performance-limiting behavior, it helps to return to the early research on group dynamics. Much of the early leader-group research stems from Freud (1959). Freud believed a group that is suddenly stripped of its leader becomes dysfunctional. Like a man with his head cut off, the leaderless group loses all ties among members and breaks apart, running crazily in all directions. W. F. Bion (1959), a tank commander turned psychoanalyst, put an interesting twist on Freud's idea of dependency and leadership. Bion went on to describe how group members develop a strong dependence on leaders, a phenomenon he called dependent group culture. According to Bion, group members will turn to leaders for direction and to get reinforcement when they experience the inevitable uncertainty associated with being part of a group.

Bion made many of his discoveries while leading a group of veterans in the psychiatric wing of a military hospital. Bion became a pioneer of group therapy methods. He recounts how he came to observe dependent group culture. After several meetings with one particular group, he began to notice that group members came to meetings ready to discuss important developments in their individual treatment plans. This seemed a promising development because the purpose of the meeting was group therapy. In other words, the shared group purpose rested in improving the mental health of individual group members through group conversation and analysis. In this group, individuals were now openly discussing their individual development, which showed progress toward the stated purpose.

Despite the promising trend, however, Bion noticed something disturbing as well. The individual group members virtually ignored other members of the group and sought the sole attention of Bion himself, the team leader. The group sessions began to look like a series of two-way conversations between the leader and each individual group member. Further, it appeared that as members of the group took turns discussing their insights, they waited patiently for Bion to dispense advice and guidance. So not only did the members seek Bion's exclusive attention, they also failed to recognize the potential contribution of other group members.

Bion became troubled by the development. After all, he had hoped that group therapy would provide a new form of self-help. What he experienced in this particular group, however, looked more like individual therapy, albeit in a group setting. Bion observed that each member of the group began to vie for his attention. Each group member thought it desirable and in fact demanded that Bion, the leader himself, dispense advice. This demand for attention from the leader meant that the group members failed to develop any kind of interdependence with other group members. No group formed because individuals depended on the leader to run the group.

The biggest problem with the emerging group dynamic came to light. This group culture of dependence caused a great deal of undesirable tension and anxiety as individual members sought ways to get the attention of the group leader and exclude other members. The tension quickly dissipated, however, if Bion jumped in and responded to the individual group member's demand. For Bion, jumping in to respond to these demands seemed the logical thing to do as it quickly released the tension. Interestingly, Bion noted that the tension quickly returned even when the issues became resolved to the satisfaction of the individual member. Simply responding to the demands failed to release the tension, save for a few moments of peace. As the tension re-emerged, group members began to resent each other. It seemed that the group never learned how to resolve issues or take action without the intervention of the leader. The problem of group dependency on the leader began to take full form.

DEPENDENCY IN TEAMS

Bion may have been the first to systematically describe the problem of group dependence in the journal *Human Relations*. The setting in which these notes were taken, a psychoanalytic group in a military hospital during World War II, may seem far away in kind and place from the inhospitable environment of Everest in 1996. Yet, Bion's notes help expose a problem that may account for the strange events on Everest. It is important to keep in mind that turning to Bion's work does not mean to imply that the members of the Everest teams were in need of psychiatric counseling. Indeed, years of observation and research on group dynamics confirm that group dependence can exist in groups where all members demonstrate good mental health. Bion's notes do, however, illuminate the psychological complexities of group behavior in general and on Everest in particular.

The important point to take away from Bion's studies is that group dependence on the leader prevents individual team members from learning to personally deal with their situation. Further, group dependency leads members to overlook the potential contribution that other group members can make to the group. As can be seen as Bion's notes take shape, groups that become so totally dependent on their leaders for advice and direction fail to gain the necessary skills and abilities to make important decisions absent the leader. A deeper look at Bion's notes illuminates three characteristics of dependent groups: helplessness, pairing, and a fight–flight response.

HELPLESSNESS

Leaders can do several things that increase dependency. In fact, leaders' words and actions themselves may be the biggest contributing factors to dependence. Leaders build dependence by encouraging members to rely only on them. Leaders build dependence by creating an environment that makes it difficult for team members to take initiative without their involvement. In this way, leaders stifle the ability of team members to take action. The problem with dependence on a leader is that team members become helpless in their efforts to effect change, realize personal goals, and develop as individuals. This occurs because the individual cannot take action without the implicit or explicit consent of the leader. Helplessness becomes harmful to the team's ability to reach its goals because it delays or outright prevents the development of the individual and the group.

Leaders Fischer and Hall made explicit that the team leaders would enforce the turnaround times during the pursuit of the summit. These two leaders chose to enforce the turnaround times themselves because they felt they, better than the team members or assistant guides, were best able to judge the circumstances. Yet, in not developing individual team members to take action and descend, the leaders unknowingly increased team member dependence on them. The problem set in when the leaders became increasingly unable to make judgments. Indeed, at times the leaders were simply unavailable to turn individual climbers around because the teams had become separated on the mountain.

PAIRING

Pairing occurs when two or more members of the group decide to pursue their own interests or goals together, without including other members of the group. When pairing occurs, the individuals begin to feel hopeful about achieving the goal. Pairing tends to allow individuals to create an overly optimistic picture of the future as they gain new hope that an idealized future can be obtained. The problem with pairing is that not all members of the group will develop the same optimism; some members will remain behind. Pairing often becomes a destructive force in groups because members begin to further alienate themselves from other members of the group. Such alienation in turn takes resources away that will benefit the group.

Take, for example, the decision by Scott Fischer's assistant guide Lopsang Jangbu to short-rope Sandy Pittman to the summit. Short-roping is usually done when individuals are too weak to climb on their own and is used to aid in their descent to safety. What was unique about the short-roping of Pittman was that one of the leaders actually dragged her up the mountain. As Jangbu short-roped Pittman up the mountain, it meant he failed to perform an expected task for the team.

Jangbu was supposed to coordinate with a member of Hall's team to fix a stretch of ropes that would make for a quicker ascent. Fixing ropes makes it easier, safer, and, most importantly, quicker for climbers to ascend a section of the mountain because a path has already been cut into the snow. Climbers clip onto a fixed rope that is attached to ice and rocks. The clip in turn is attached to a harness that wraps around the midsection or possibly the full body of the climber. By clipping his or her harness onto the fixed rope via a special clip, the climber has less to fear should he or she stumble since the fixed rope serves as a kind of safety line. Recall that Jangbu was a paid guide and had specific responsibilities that other members of the team, by virtue of the fact they were paying clients, did not have.

When Jangbu failed to show up early in the morning before the other climbers had arrived, a member of Hall's team refused to fix the ropes alone. Only when the rest of the team arrived at the section of the climb did they realize the ropes had not been fixed. One of Fischer's assistant guides, Neil Beidleman, and other members of the team fixed ropes when Jangbu failed to arrive. The fact that Jangbu and Pittman "paired" off and he carried her up the mountain meant that other members of the team did not have all the available resources.

FIGHT–FLIGHT RESPONSES

A sure sign of a dependent group occurs when a group displays "fight or flight" behaviors. Fight occurs when individuals show hostility toward the leader and other members of the team for not meeting individual needs. On the other hand, teams may enter a state of flight as group members flee the scene and disengage with the team and its goals. The fight or flight responses emerge from a dislike, even hatred, of the leader. Both fight and flight responses arise as team members seek to find some hope in achieving their goal.

Of all the possible group dependencies, fight–flight appears less prevalent in the Everest teams in question. The South African team may have displayed elements of fight–flight: flight could be seen as nearly all the team members fled the team and left the goal of summiting behind. As a result of this flight, the South African team virtually disintegrated under the leadership of Woodall.

Taken together, helplessness, pairing, and fight–flight provide indicators of team members' dependence on leadership. It is important to remember that dependence on leaders plays an important role: it lowers the anxiety of group members and provides identification with a leader who is seen as infallible. Yet, dependence on leadership has drawbacks. Dependence limits the ability of team members to learn from their own actions, and ultimately both individual and team learning becomes stifled. Individuals fail to learn because they depend too much on the leader to define their identity and actions. At the same time, individuals fail to accept that they have anything to learn from other members of the team.

LOSS OF TEAM IDENTITY

The ultimate results of dependence on the leader is an overall loss of a shared identity as a team. The team dependence prevalent on Everest resulted in an inability to function without the heavy hand of the leader. Dependency prevents teams from functioning because the team's identity rests in the personality and charisma of the leader, not with the goal of the team. Team dependence leads to a loss of team identity as individuals pursued their goals without the shared team-level goal. By most accounts, American guide Fischer demonstrated the least authoritative style of the guides on Everest. More of a motivator than an authoritarian, Fischer seems an unlikely leader to build dysfunctional dependence in his teams. Yet, Fischer promoted the kind of rugged individualism common among mountaineers. While this rugged self-dependence may be effective in certain types of climbs, the demands of a commercial expedition team require greater attention to interpersonal skills and leader–follower relations. Fischer's catch phrase—"It's attitude not altitude" (Boukreev and DeWalt, 1997)—used to address his increasingly weak and sick team members was emblematic of how bravado may have overshadowed developmental thinking and further built the dependence of the team members on their leader.

Similarly, Taiwanese team leader Gau had earlier abandoned his fallen and soon-to-be-dead teammate. Gau continued his climb without the team member and left the Breashears team to carry down the dead body. One New Zealand team member demonstrated an almost alarming lack of team identity as she focused on self-reliance rather than team effort. She stated that a successful climb resulted from "self-reliance, on making critical decisions and dealing with the consequences." Ultimately, she argued that success would rely "on personal responsibility" (Krakauer, 1997a, p. 168). Assistant guide Beidleman, in his analysis of events, showed the pervasiveness of the teamlessness that season on Everest when he stated, "Sure, we made little mistakes all along the way. But looking back, none of it went to cause the death of Scott Fischer." Krakauer lamented the lack of teamwork as well in his comment, "I felt disconnected from the climbers around me—emotionally, spiritually, physically.... We were a team in name only" (Krakauer, 1997a, p. 163).

More concrete examples of the lack of team identity also existed on Everest. Important evidence includes the decision by team members not to rope together during many sections of the climb. Typically, climbers clip ropes to their body harnesses and then clip these ropes. Roping entails clipping climbers together so that if one team member slips or falls, the fall is more likely to become arrested by the weight of the additional climbers. For example, if a climber remains clipped in her rope and falls into a crevasse in the ice, she need not worry quite as much. The other climbers attached to the ropes can pull her out. By the same token, however, the other team members can also be dragged down the crevasse with her if they do not react fast enough to arrest her fall. The important connection between roping together and teamwork is that roping serves as a kind of metaphor for team interdependence since all members carry a common fate when roped together. The fact that the teams chose not to rope together provides further evidence that the members of the climbing teams lacked team effort (Kayes, 2004a).

As destructive as team dependence can be in limiting a team's performance, many teams can function just fine under a condition of team
dependence. Team dependence does not always prevent a team from
achieving its goal, particularly when the team's goal is one that requires
effort and not knowledge, structure and not adaptability. But when a
team requires the ability to respond to changing circumstances, like the
situations faced on Everest, team dependence can be deadly for teamwork.
No team, however, can function for very long if it remains dependent
when its leader is overcome with complexity.

The complexity of leadership

One limit of relying on leadership lies in the tendency of dependent teams
to drag down the team and decrease the team's ability to successfully
realize its goals. Another limit to leadership is the ability of leaders themselves. Leaders often fail to understand the complexity of the problems
they face. Leaders' limited ability to see the complexity of a situation
results in the establishment of goals that are too narrow to adequately
address the problem faced. Without a complex and extensive knowledge
of the situation being faced, leaders often misjudge situations and blunder
into problems. Leadership, after all, requires responding to a complex
mix of psychological and task-related demands. Short the ability to adapt
and change to these demands, leaders may find themselves unable to
cope with the situation.

Robert Kegan (1994), a noted development psychologist, articulated
this problem. Kegan believes that leaders often get "in over their heads."
Kegan, like others, realizes that learning does not stop after adoles-
cence. Kegan, as a constructivist–developmental psychologist, suggests
that leaders do not just passively act in an environment. Rather, leaders
construct, or actively participate in their world. Leadership is an inten-
tional process, one where leaders create, rather than just simply respond
to their environment. According to Kegan, in order to understand leadership, we need a better understanding of how leaders learn to understand their environment. Kegan describes learning as the process whereby
a leader begins to better understand his or her relationship to others
as well as the context in which those relationships exist. In order to
navigate this complex interpersonal process, a leader must understand
the contingencies, subjectivities, and uncertainties that lie at the core of
these interpersonal relationships.

Kegan can be understood along with other humanist psychologists,
such as Abraham Maslow, who believe in the potential of individuals to

influence and guide their own successful goal-setting and achievement. If we take Kegan's ideas to heart, the fundamental question that can be asked about the limits of leadership goes something like this: What are the things that are keeping the leader from realizing the goals he or she wants to achieve? Notice this question changes the focus from what the leader is doing to achieve the goal to what the leader is doing to keep the goal from being achieved.

On Everest, Hall and Fischer could be seen as doing a number of things that, in retrospect, prevented the teams from getting to the summit and back down successfully. For example, Fischer insisted on following behind his team members, which resulted in Fischer being separated from the team's members. Yet, Fischer failed to provide the team members with the necessary support to make decisions themselves. Likewise, Hall's authoritative style prevented many of the team members from making decisions on their own.

On both teams, assistant guides may have also taken actions that prevented the teams from being successful. By short-roping Pittman, Jangbu took valuable resources from the group, including failing to fix the ropes to make ascent and descent go more quickly. Boukreev decided to summit without oxygen and alone, leaving individual clients to fend for themselves. These acts could be seen as limiting actions that may have actually led to the destructive pursuit of goals.

As can be seen on Everest, the actions of leaders may have prevented, rather than facilitated, the achievement of goals. In a sense, leaders engage in self-defeating behaviors. These self-defeating behaviors emerged not because the leaders intentionally wanted to sabotage their team's achievement of goals. The leaders were not aware that these behaviors would contribute to disaster. Instead, they engaged in self-defeating behaviors because they failed to recognize that the situation involved multiple competing goals.

COMPETING GOALS

To better understand why leaders engage in self-defeating behaviors, it helps to understand that most situations require multiple goals. At times, these goals are in direct competition with each other. More explicitly, competing goals describe how leaders face two often conflicting and mutually exclusive goals at the same time. These dual goals are often internalized; the leaders themselves are not aware of them. These competing goals create dilemmas for leaders: by trying to preserve both goals, the leader ends up achieving neither. The way to resolve such dilemmas is to understand the underlying assumptions that keep the leader from realizing her goals. A couple of things to consider about these competing goals include the following:

▶ All leaders hold these competing goals. Hall and Fischer may have wanted to get all the clients to the summit but at the same time realized that not all clients could get up safely. Thus, they made trade-offs between getting some clients up safely and took chances with others. The goal of getting everyone to the top was in conflict with the goal of keeping everyone safe.
▶ Leaders want to seem "rational"—nonparadoxical, noncontradictory in beliefs, and consistent in thinking. Hall and Fischer did not want to express doubt about getting members to the top safely, so they expressed only confidence in getting to the summit, not doubts about getting back down. This kept their message about success consistent. Other statements by climbers, such as "if only the weather holds, we will have success" allowed climbers to ignore any inner contradictions.

Kegan helps uncover the second limitation of leadership on Everest. Too often, leaders fail to recognize that they hold competing goals and this causes them to ignore one goal at the expense of the other goal.

COMPETING COMMITMENTS ON "K2"

This interplay between competing goals was brought to its dramatic height in Patrick Meyers' (1983) play *K2*, about a climbing team trapped on the world's second tallest mountain. One climber, Harold, was severely wounded and unable to descend. The uninjured climber, Taylor, was faced with two competing commitments: descend alone and live with the knowledge of abandoning his teammate or stay on the mountain and perish along with him. After lengthy discussions, Taylor and Harold decided that Taylor will descend alone to tell the story of their struggle. Of course, the struggle Taylor told was not one of a successful mountain-climbing team, but rather of one that "messed up" (p. 36) and the struggle to balance his commitment to a friend trapped on a mountain with his commitment to friends and family below.

The K2 story resembles the circumstances faced independently by guides Fischer and Hall on Everest. Hall was helping client Doug Hansen, who had collapsed near the summit and was unable to descend unaided. The prior year, Hall had turned Hansen around just a few hundred feet shy of the summit because he feared not getting down safely. This year, determining which commitment to respond to was not so clear. Similarly, Fischer was found roped to the body of Taiwanese climber

Gau, which suggests he was helping the climber descend. Although we do not know exactly what these struggles entailed, it seems reasonable to see similarities between the situation dramatized on K2 and that faced by the Everest guides. Both faced competing commitments between getting other climbers down safely and ensuring their own survival to tell about it.

One way to understand the nature of competing goals faced by leaders is to consider both the task and interpersonal goals inherent in leadership itself.

DUAL DEMANDS OF LEADERSHIP: TASK AND INTERPERSONAL

Managing complex and difficult logistics of an expedition is only one of the demands on Everest. As anthropologist Sherry Ortner reminds us, social and psychological demands also play an important part in effective leadership in mountaineering. She writes:

> Once the group gets to the mountain, differences of personality, nationality, climbing values and many other things are enormously magnified by the close quarters, the stressful physical conditions, and the difficulty of the task. Although physical abilities, technical skills, and equipment are fundamental to success, the job of climbing the mountain involves as well an enormous component of interpersonal relations. (Ortner, 1999, p. 11)

Freed Bales (1958) and his colleagues at Harvard verified nearly half a century ago that leaders face dual demands. They wanted to understand what demands leaders actually face in groups. Bales set up an experimental lab to observe undergraduate students in ad hoc groups working on a short, time-bound problem. The teams had the same work as a project team or task force common in organizations. The students would sit in groups in a room with one-way mirrors and discuss open-ended questions. Bales did not assign a formal leader in the groups but waited for a leader to emerge naturally.

The studies revealed some interesting results. Two kinds of leaders emerged in each group. One type of leader was task oriented. The task-oriented leader focused the group on accomplishing the stated goal of the team, for the teams tried to solve the problem that was given to them at the beginning of each session. Second, a process-oriented leader emerged. The process-oriented leader focused on the group's interpersonal interactions. Bales termed the process-oriented leader the "maintenance" leader because this person maintained the sense of group identity and maintained the spirits of the group when members got discouraged. Overall, the groups spent about 60–70 percent of their time on task-oriented behaviors and about 30–40 percent of their time on maintenance behaviors.

The researchers found that which particular individual performed each of the two leadership roles varied from group to group but that the same individuals seemed to play either a maintenance or a task leader role in almost every group. Only in about 5 percent of the cases did one member assume both a task and a maintenance role. In other words, certain individuals seemed to emerge as both process and task leaders, but this did not happen frequently. From these studies, we can conclude that leadership requires a dual set of goals—task goals and interpersonal goals. Some goals require task skills and other goals require interpersonal skills, but most goals, at least most complex and challenging goals faced by leaders in real-world situations, require a combination of both. What becomes so critical for understanding the limits of leadership is that few leaders (less than 5 percent, it seems) can fulfill both task and interpersonal demands of leadership.

Bales' research has been extremely influential in leadership studies and spurred the creation of many tools and models still in use to train and assess leadership. Most of these models and tools suggest that effective leadership requires scoring high on both interpersonal and task-oriented behaviors. The idea behind this was that the best leaders were "high-high" leaders. That is to say, they scored high on both interpersonal and task leadership duties. Years of study and observation, however, reveal that few leaders are capable of demonstrating a strong orientation toward both task and interpersonal issues. This is not surprising based on Bales' studies.

The notion that leaders need to cultivate both task and interpersonal skills confirms that leadership requires a variety of complex and divergent skills. Taken together, the idea of competing commitments and the dual demands of leadership confirm that few individuals possess the skills to accomplish all the tasks necessary to achieve goals. Herein lies the paradox of leadership. When an individual enters a team, he or she does so to accomplish a goal that could not be achieved alone. Oftentimes, and this was the case on Everest, entering such a group only breeds dependence on the leader. The leader, not the group, becomes the psychological focus of the team member, and the team member becomes dependent on the leader to accomplish the goal. The more dependent the team member becomes on the leader, the less likely he or she will learn what is necessary to accomplish the goal. The result is that the team fails to accomplish the very goal it sets out to achieve.

This chapter reaches the conclusion that leadership involves such a complex and diverse set of tasks that it is nearly impossible to demand all these necessary skills and abilities from one person. In most complex and changing situations, leadership requires a team of leaders and not just an individual. Everest team leaders Fischer, Hall, and Gau, although experienced, strong, and level-headed, could not reasonably respond to the complexity of the situation on Everest. The leaders were in over their heads. Further, many teams, like those on Everest, can become dependent on their leaders for direction and guidance. Being dependent on a leader who is in over his head creates a disastrous mix during the pursuit of difficult and challenging goals. Unfortunately, this is exactly the situation that emerged on Everest as authoritative leaders took control of the group's decision-making.

Goalodicy emerges as teams become dependent on limited leaders. This is one of the most important mechanisms that led to the Everest disaster. Leadership may be one of the most important factors leading to destructive goal pursuit. While a dependent group describes one of the psychological principles of goalodicy, it is often difficult to recognize. Better indicators that goalodicy has taken over are needed. The next chapter outlines six warning signs.

Learning points

▶ Leadership has certain limitations. In many cases, like Everest, leadership can facilitate the onset of goalodicy by identifying too closely with the future as yet unachieved goal.

▶ One important limitation of leadership is that team members can become dependent on leaders. Oftentimes, leaders encourage team members to be dependent because it reaffirms the value of the leader. Other times, leaders unknowingly create this dependence by not developing their followers to be autonomous. Dependence limits learning of team members and prevents teams from forming and working toward a common goal.

▶ A second limitation of leadership is that leaders often try to take on goals that are too complex for an individual to handle alone. Leadership involves a complex mix of task- and interpersonal-related goals. In addition, leaders face demands that are often too complex for all outcomes to be achieved.

▶ The result of leadership in teams is that it creates a paradox where individuals become dependent on leaders to help them achieve goals but leaders themselves stifle the ability of the team to accomplish the goal.

Learning questions

▶ How did the actions of the leaders on Everest make their team members more dependent on the leader? For example, how did Hall's declaration that he and he alone would be enforcing the turnaround time take authority away from individual team members?

▶ How did the actions of the guides or team leaders encourage goalodicy?

▶ Think of a leader whom you have admired. The person can be either someone from your life or someone you have admired from afar. What specific actions or characteristics did that leader show? Did the leader create dependence in any way? Did the leader increase autonomy of followers?

▶ Think of some ways that leaders can learn to manage complexity. For example, how can delegating tasks or improving individual team members' abilities help accomplish goals?

5 Warning Signs: Indicators of Goalodicy

In the midst of pursuing your goal, it becomes difficult to think about why you are pursuing the goal—your initial motivation and why achieving the goal has become so important. You don't have time to think about the past; you can only focus your attention on what it will take to reach the goal. The goal you have set, summiting Everest, is simple and clear. No one will doubt that you have reached the summit. In fact, at home and now here on the isolated mountain, there is little doubt; everyone seems to think that you will achieve the goal. Indeed, you have had to counsel those who fail to see your progress to this point as anything less than spectacular. You counsel them that they fail to see your strength and they fail to recognize your progress up the mountain so far. In fact, their negativity only makes the goal more clear. Any obstacles that may rest between you and reaching the summit seem small in comparison to the ecstasy you will experience once the summit is achieved.

Some naysayer even cautions that you may abandon your goal on the final push to the summit, but you know that is unlikely. You respond in the following way: How can you abandon your goal when you are actively pursuing the summit? That logic doesn't make sense to everyone; it seems circular—you are using your goal of reaching the summit to justify your continued pursuit. But to you and many of those around you, this response makes perfect sense. It is not just the summit you hope to reach but yourself that you want to define. Achieving the summit carries a kind of destiny. The naysayer sees something in your behavior, recognizing that it may be a warning sign of goalodicy.

This chapter outlines six warning signs of goalodicy and presents evidence for their existence on Everest. Each of the warning signs represents an indicator that the goalodicy process has begun to take hold in a person, group, or organization. In addition, each warning sign helps clarify the deeper psychological mechanisms at work during destructive goal pursuit.

Narrowly defined goal

Setting goals, especially specific and narrow goals, can lead to problems when conditions require learning. For example, when a team sets a specific goal, the team may become unable to adapt to changes in the environment. Remember the participants in the stock price simulation mentioned in Chapter 3. The researcher created two distinct groups. One group tried to achieve specific and narrow goals, while the other group tried to achieve the more general goal of "doing their best." The group that held the general goal outperformed the group that held specific goals. It seems that in some cases, like when the task at hand is dynamic and complex, general goals are preferred to specific goals.

If the Everest teams defined their goal narrowly, such as getting to the top as efficiently as possible, then goal-setting would likely contribute to the problems they faced. The following description of climbing Everest, provided by a journalist reporting the events, provides an example of how a narrowly defined goal might limit a climber's perception of the complexities required of reaching the summit:

> The South Col, the site of the highest camp on the Nepalese side of the mountain, is at 7,906 meters [25,938 feet]. The summit is 8,848 meters [29,029 feet]. Climbing 90 meters [295 feet] per hour you should gain the difference in about 10 hours. Add a couple of rest stops and some time to enjoy the view on top, and you're looking at 12 hours up. Six hours for the descent makes it 18 hours round trip. Then there's the oxygen. At an average flow of two liters per minute, a bottle will last six hours. You'll carry two—with regulator and mask, they'll total maybe 15 pounds—and your Sherpa support climbers will carry a third for you. That gives you 18 hours of total climbing time. (Kennedy, 1996, pp. 96–97)

Eighteen hours of climbing time. The problem with such a statement is that it has the potential to lull climbers into thinking that all they need to do is put in 18 hours of effort and the goal will be achieved. Eighteen hours of climbing time says nothing about the tough emotions that will be encountered on the way up. Eighteen hours says nothing about how to respond to dilemmas that may arise. Eighteen hours says nothing about managing the contingencies that will arise during the climb. Eighteen hours says nothing about how to abandon your goal when you are minutes away from the goal but well past your 18 hours of climbing time. Eighteen hours only provides a starting point.

The best climbers, those lured by goals but moderated by sense, take another angle on what it takes to achieve the summit. The best climbers include contingency, emotion, the possibility of indecision, and dilemma in their view of reaching the summit. Eighteen hours may serve as the starting point, but beyond that, reaching the summit and getting back down require an understanding of human emotions. As climber Ed Viesturs expresses, success rests more on the emotional pull of reaching the summit. He describes the decision to abandon a goal in the following way:

> When you're up there, you've spent years of training, months of preparation, and weeks of climbing and you're within view of the summit, and you know, you have—in the back of your mind you're telling yourself, "We should turn around 'cause we're late, we're gonna run out of oxygen," but you see the summit, and it draws you there. And a lot of people—it's so magnetic that they tend to break their rules and they go to the summit—and, on a good day, you can get away with it. And on a bad day, you'll die. (Viesturs, quoted in Rose, 1998)

Viesturs' comments are more in line with learning and adaptation than the blind pursuit of goals. His logic suggests three attributes to goals not expressed by the 18 hours model:

▶ Challenging goals often require multiple, often contradictory solutions (e.g., the lure of the summit versus knowing one should turn around), often expressed through the negative or contradictory demands inherent in an activity.
▶ Achieving goals relies as much on the emotional, subjective, and potentially ambiguous nature of the solution (e.g., the "lure," being "drawn" there, when to "break the rules") as it does on rational processes such as counting the hours to ascend to the summit of Everest from the final camp.
▶ Achieving difficult goals requires responding to the contingency of the situation in relation to prior experience (e.g., "on a good day, you can get away with it. . . . On a bad day, you'll die").

Too many times, mountain climbers defined their goals narrowly, like achieving the summit of the mountain with little consideration for getting back down. But as experienced climbers know, "the top is only half way there . . . most people die on the way down" (Krakauer, quoted on ABC News, 1996a). Narrowly defined goals work just fine if reaching the goal is a matter of sustained effort. If reaching the goal requires learning, like it does to reach the summit of Everest, then a more broadly defined view of the goal and how to reach it must be achieved.

Public expectation

Another warning sign of goalodicy involves public expectation. Destructive goal pursuit is more likely when the failure to accomplish the goal would be met by public perception of failure. Publicity for Everest climbs became an increasingly necessary part of climbing. Publicity came in many forms. Expeditions sought corporate sponsorships to help defray expedition costs such as expensive climbing gear, support staff such as porters and guides, and increasingly expensive climbing permits. Nation states often provided support for teams as a way to build national pride, and individuals sought the attention of the media to launch lucrative speaking and public appearance engagements.

Few expedition leaders showed the public relations skills of Scott Fischer. Earlier in 1996, Fischer had orchestrated a live broadcast of his summit of Kilimanjaro, the highest peak in Africa. On Kilimanjaro, or "Kili" as some call it, Fischer led a group of deep-pocketed executives up the peak. By most measures, Kili did not pose any great technical diffi- culties for climbers. Any reasonably conditioned person, with the right motivation and the ability to withstand the discomfort of the extreme elevation change in a short period of time, had a high likelihood of success. Summiting Kili looks more like a goal that requires sustained effort rather than learning.

By most measures, the Kili climb resulted in a publicity success, as Fischer continued to attract high-profile clients to his company, Moun- tain Madness, even when the expeditions faced more difficult terrain and required greater technical expertise. Fischer's team member Sandy Hill Pittman was the kind of client who, if she was successful, could create great publicity for the relatively unknown enterprise of mountain climbing. Pittman drew attention from the start, since she filed daily logs of her pursuits with the NBC website. At one point, rumors floated that Martha Stewart herself would greet Pittman at base camp upon her return from the summit. Although Stewart never actually showed up, the idea gained much attention.

Rob Hall's team carried its own publicity burden that season. Jon Krakauer's assignment was to report on the commercialization of climbing as well as participate in the summit attempt. Krakauer climbed on assignment for *Outside*, a monthly magazine popular among actual and armchair climbers alike. Krakauer joined Hall's team to write about his experience for an upcoming issue. With his dark and tame beard, Krakauer could almost pass for Hall's brother. In contrast to Hall, however, Krakauer carried the demeanor of a poet—he was quiet, reserved, and more likely to sit back and observe events than to try to determine them. Over the years, Krakauer achieved the status of a strong all-around climber who had a special gift for explaining the detailed drama of a climb in retrospect. He published his account of the 1996 events a year later in a book entitled *Into Thin Air*, which remained on the best-seller list for over a year.

Krakauer and Hall became teammates mostly by chance. The editors at *Outside* magazine had originally negotiated with a team organized by American Scott Fischer's Mountain Madness expedition and adventure company. Editors negotiated a last-minute deal with Hall to provide a deep discount for Krakauer. The discounted rate ensured that Krakauer would be along with the Hall team and likely provide some additional publicity for Hall to compensate for the lost revenue.

Some observers of the events point to these publicity-driven activities as well as some of the more business-oriented activities as a fundamental change in the nature of mountain climbing. For example, Elmes and Barry (1999) believe a variety of changes in the nature of mountain climbing may have contributed to the disaster. They argue that the commercialization of the mountain-climbing industry has allowed less-experienced climbers access to the highest and most difficult peaks. Because these climbers lack the experience and safety knowledge, climbers are more likely to experience disaster and are less likely to know how to respond.

High-altitude mountain climbers have always displayed a flair for publicity and business savvy. Almost since the beginning of expedition mountain climbing, leaders have used publicity for a variety of reasons. Even Edmond Hillary and Tenzing Norgay's first successful ascent of Mt Everest in 1953 became media fodder almost immediately. The earliest full-scale expeditions to summit Everest bore striking resemblances to the expeditions in 1996 in many ways. As one historian concedes, these early

> ambitious expeditions demanded large sums of money, and wealthy patrons were in short supply after [World War II]. However, from the first, attempts to climb Everest were supported by *The Times*, which paid substantial sums for the dispatches sent back from the mountain. It was the first move in a progress, or regress, which was eventually to see major expeditions financed by popular press, by radio and television, and by advanced payments for book rights—all steps which eventually tended to transform a sport into a special branch of the entertainment industry. (Clark, 1976, p. 167)

The influx of celebrity climbers and the Internet posting of the daily events on Everest in 1996 seemed only a modern-day, high-tech version of the age-old desire for recognition of a difficult goal accomplished. Publicity and business may have played a role in 1996, but overall, the 1996 climbers were little different than climbers of many earlier expeditions in their desire for publicity.

What was different in 1996 was the increased expectation of a successful ascent. Indeed, evidence that there was great expectation came from the news dispatches. The American team leader, Scott Fischer, boasted of "having the big 'E' [Everest] all figured out." This confidence spilled over to his team members, as one of Pittman's logs suggested a confidence in her ability to achieve difficult goals and helped set public expectations of an impeding successful summit. One log proposed that "as long as the weather holds, we will have success" and one of the assistant guides told another climbing expedition that "We expect to get everyone up."

Face-saving behavior

Another important indicator that goal pursuit has gone too far lies in the notion of face-saving behavior. Generally, "face-saving" refers to efforts to maintain dignity or prestige, to avoid admitting to something embarrassing. In the context of goalodicy, face-saving behavior occurs when a person engaged in goal pursuit seeks to maintain his identity, even in the face of contradictory evidence. Such behavior feeds public expectation: the goal seeker wants to maintain public respectability and belief that the goal will be achieved, even if the pursuit has gone too far or achievement of the goal is far less certain. Rationalization is involved here as well: a goal setter may change rationalizations for action, but the same actions seem to be taken—and face-saving behavior involves explaining and justifying the course of action rather than amending it.

Michael Roberto (2002), who has written a case study of events, proposes that the Everest teams lacked the ability, or the know-how, to challenge the dominant viewpoint held by the group. The group engaged in face-saving behaviors by deferring to leadership, failing to question the ability of leaders, and effectively becoming dependent on leaders to make life-and-death decisions.

Idealized future

One sure sign that goalodicy has arrived rests in the belief, held among group members, that current problems, limitations, or setbacks will resolve themselves in the future. Belief in an idealized future serves a psychological purpose. The belief helps people endure present hardship. Belief that problems will be resolved in the future provides a form of justification for enduring current hardships and continuing in the face of set backs.

An idealized future may provide hope and direction during many difficult times. Taken to an extreme, overidealization of the future can blind teams and their leader to the realities of the present. This reliance on the future may be particularly troublesome during times of crisis because crisis situations require acute attention to the present, not dreamy-eyed ideals of a future utopia.

On Everest, there were a number of indicators of an idealized future. Many of the climbers expressed the need to reach the top in order to be fulfilled as a person. The most dramatic example of this was Doug Hansen. A client of Hall, in 1995, Hansen had abandoned his pursuit a few hundred feet from the summit. Hall had turned Hansen around. In 1996, both Hall and Hansen had an incentive to reach the top, but Hansen seemed to believe reaching his goal would answer many of his problems.

Likewise, Bruce Herrod, the South African team member, had placed high hopes in what could be accomplished after returning. Some had argued that Herrod had hoped that a successful summit would revive his career as an adventurer. Many individuals believe that a successful summit will change their lives by bringing them fame and fortune on the lecture circuit as it has for many climbers. Those who successfully summit Everest do not always realize the future that they idealized, but the vision of an idealized future does point to the onset of destructive goal pursuit.

Goal-driven justification

If belief in an idealized future allows leaders to ignore current limitations, such beliefs also allow leaders, and the teams that follow them, to justify current action in terms of the future idealized state. The goals help define what this future state will look like. Like the face-saving behaviors and idealized futures mentioned above, the future goal provides justification for present setbacks, limitations, or problems. The justification for continued pursuit involves a logic that goes something like this: "I can endure present hardships because once I achieve my goal, these hardships will go away. I don't have to worry about my current problems because these problems will go away once the goal has been achieved." Goal-setting is common parlance among achievement seekers because the language of goals fuels the pursuit of achievement.

The limitation of goal justification is that it also fuels the pursuit of goals well beyond the reasonable. Goal-driven justification describes a kind of ends justifying the means logic. Future desired states provide a plausible justification of action. Unfortunately, goal-driven justification becomes a reinforcing loop where goals both ignite action in a certain direction and fuel their action. In many high-achieving individuals and teams, such high achievement has few drawbacks. But in some scenarios, particularly those situations that require novel thinking, goal-driven practice can explode into fiasco.

Achieving destiny

In many cases, people pursue goals to destructive consequences because they believe that achieving the goal is destiny. When goals become destiny, few options other than achieving the goal enter the mind of those pursuing the goal. The goal seeker begins to believe that fortune is on one's side and thus obtaining the goal cannot possibly be derailed. The idea that achieving a goal is providence tends to block out contradictory information that suggests the goal cannot be reached.

On Everest, several comments show that the teams thought they were achieving destiny. Pittman's web log that "if the weather holds, we will have success" and Fischer's belief that his and other expeditions that season were "setting protocol" for future expeditions set the tone that the teams were destined to reach the summit.

All of these warning signs existed on Everest to some degree or another. These warning signs suggest that the Everest teams had fallen prey to the problem of goalodicy. In addition, the warning signs not only indicate that goalodicy had set in, but suggest how leaders facilitated the onset of goalodicy. The destructive pursuit of goals does not happen on its own. Rather, leaders and their followers play an active role in identifying too closely with an as yet unachieved goal.

The warning signs provide six indicators of how leaders help maintain the belief in the future goal. Leaders and their groups play an important part in the emergence and the maintenance of goalodicy. The next chapter examines how leaders and team members work together, often unknowingly, to build and maintain a team culture of destructive goal pursuit.

Learning points

Warning signs that goalodicy has emerged include:

▶ the acceptance of a narrowly defined goal
▶ a prevailing public expectation that achieving the goal is eminent
▶ face-saving behavior displayed by the team or individual
▶ the idealization of a future in which no or few problems exist
▶ pursuit that is justified by the goal itself and not other logic, and
▶ the feeling, shared among team members, that achieving the goal is destiny.

Learning questions

▶ Can you think of any additional warning signs that might exist for goalodicy that were not mentioned above?

▶ Take some time to think through the six warning signs of goalodicy in relation to a goal you have set for yourself. You might refer back to a goal you considered in the learning questions of prior chapters. Have any of the six warning signs of goalodicy existed during pursuit of your goal?

6 The Recipe for Disaster: Seven Steps Leading to Goalodicy

Today you set out to achieve your goal, the summit of Everest. You have now spent weeks climbing up and down the side of the world's highest mountain, setting up ropes, establishing continually higher camps, and working through the treacherous pillars of ice in the Khumbu ice fall. At base camp you are now taking about 20 breaths a minute, and your body can barely stay hydrated. You need to eat over 6,000 calories a day just to maintain your weight.

It is 10:30 in the evening of the final push to the summit. You just arrived at this high camp a few hours ago. You now rest at 27,600 feet above sea level. The location where you first caught summit fever seems a world away. At this altitude you take nearly 30 breaths a minute and still fail to gulp enough air to fill your lungs. No motor vehicles can make it here, and no helicopters have attempted a rescue at these heights. No person can carry you at this altitude. You are on your own to get up the mountain. You've been breathing bottled oxygen regularly to refresh your lungs. Your body cannot adjust to this altitude; you simply must stay the course and force your body to continue.

You drag your body from the warmth of your sleeping bag and drink whatever melted snow is left in your cup. Your headlamp is already attached. The headlamp will guide you through the first several hours of your ascent during the dark. When the sun rises, you will be guided by the mountain peak itself. You crawl out of your tent, excited about your final push to the summit but exhausted at the same time. You know you will have to summon every last bit of strength to achieve your goal, but there is no turning back now. Perseverance and effort brought you this far, and you need to draw on these qualities to get you the final 2,000 feet to your goal.

After a quick pep talk from your guide and his assistants, you begin the final push. You are not roped together with your teammates. You have talked about a turnaround time of no later than 2:00 p.m. You know the importance of the turnaround time. A 2:00 p.m. turnaround time will give you over 14 hours to get to the summit and 5 or 6 hours to get back down before it turns completely dark. But the 2:00 p.m. turnaround time is not fixed; that time only serves as a guideline. You know that your guides will tell you when exactly to turn around. You figure you will ascend quickly after reaching the summit. With the fixed ropes set across various points of the route, you should reach the summit by about 11:00 a.m. anyway. This vision of the summit keeps you moving, but at the moment, every bit of energy goes to putting one foot in front of the other and keeping your thinking straight. Achieving your goal is less than 12 hours away.

Chapters 3, 4, and 5 pieced together factors that led to the disaster on Everest and concluded that destructive goal pursuit may be to blame. Specifically, Chapter 3 illustrated how goal-setting, under certain conditions, may result in undesirable outcomes such as unethical behavior or unintended outcomes. Goals may even fuel failure in the face of ill-defined tasks. A name was given to this phenomenon, goalodicy, and some of the psychological and sociological mechanisms underlying the concept were explored. Chapter 4 showed how dysfunctional dependence on leaders and the difficulty of managing human dilemmas may foster goalodicy. Chapter 5 reviewed six warning signs of goalodicy.

This chapter builds on these ideas to suggest a recipe for how goalodicy develops and takes hold of a group. The chapter begins by contrasting Everest with another disaster, the death of 13 wildland firefighters at Mann Gulch. Comparing the Mann Gulch disaster to Everest highlights two key facets of goalodicy. First, teams continue to pursue goals because the goal provides an identity. Thus, goalodicy provides a way to maintain a desired identity in the face of contradictory events. Second, goalodicy can be understood as the opposite of writer's block. As a kind of "reverse writer's block," goalodicy describes how a team becomes unable to abandon a goal. The team continues to pursue the goal well beyond what is reasonable.

The second section of the chapter describes goalodicy as a barrier to learning. The section presents a seven-step recipe for how learning breaks down in teams and describes how these steps emerged on Everest. Goalodicy is described as the intersection of three variables: a narrowly defined goal, a dependent group, and the emergence of an ill-defined problem. The emergence of these three events fosters the breakdown of learning in teams.

The problem of identity

The problem of self-identity is not just a problem for the young. It is a problem all the time. Perhaps *the* problem. It should haunt old age, and when it no longer does it should tell you that you are dead. (Maclean, 1992, p. vii)

To understand the destructive pursuit of goals, we can start by looking at Maclean's words. The search for identity plays a central part in the destructive pursuit of goals. Two different disasters had contrasting problems related to identity. In Mann Gulch, the deaths of 13 smokejumpers in the foothills of the Montana countryside shows how identity can quickly disintegrate in the face of a growing threat, how identity can "collapse" and events can quickly take over a team. In contrast, the Everest incident shows how teams get burned by close identification with a distant goal, how holding onto an identity too long can draw teams into a disaster of their own making.

COLLAPSE OF IDENTITY IN THE MANN GULCH DISASTER

In 1949, 15 firefighters parachuted into the dry forest of Montana. Their goal entailed containing and eventually extinguishing a wildland fire. By most standards they faced a routine fire. The firefighters, or smoke-jumpers as they are called because they parachute out of a plane into the smoke of the fire, landed near the fire. The team met up with a forest ranger who had already begun to fight the fire. The crew ate dinner and began to take their positions. But as they delayed their engagement with the fire, it began to spread. In the foothills of Montana, fire spreads quickly in the thick and dry brush. What appeared to be a routine fire quickly and decisively overwhelmed the crew. Less than 2 hours after the smokejumpers landed, 13 of the initial firefighters, including the forest ranger, were overtaken by the fire and died.

This incident, known by the name of its location, "The Mann Gulch Disaster," haunted Norman Maclean (1992), the former University of Chicago professor best known for his book-turned-movie, *A River Runs Through It*. Maclean spent decades piecing together events, interviewing survivors and members of the smokejumpers' families, poring over official documents, and downright obsessing over the incident. Maclean's painstaking re-creation and analysis of the events provides a template for those interested in learning from the misfortunes of others; in fact, one reason his work is important to the present discussion is because it marks a systematic attempt to understand the psychology of disaster.

Karl Weick, a well-known social psychologist, reanalyzed Maclean's work in order to build a better understanding of the psychology of identity. Using Maclean's analysis, Weick (1993) concluded that the smokejumpers on Mann Gulch experienced a breakdown in their ability to make sense of their environment. The crew of smokejumpers did not expect the fire to grow as quickly as it did. As the men took time to eat dinner before taking on the fire, they demonstrated confidence in their ability to handle the fire. This confidence eventually led to their demise as they quickly became overwhelmed by the growing complexity of the situation they faced.

The complexity of the environment quickly began to surpass the ability of the crew members to manage it. Weick believes that the crew members lost their sense of individual and group identity. Since the group could no longer make sense of the new situation in which they found themselves, the smokejumpers could no longer make sense of their environment, their task, and ultimately themselves. Their identity collapsed at the very moment that they needed it to help them get out of their mess. Weick terms this sudden loss of identity a "cosmology episode." A cosmology episode entails a breakdown of both the ability to recognize oneself in a particular situation as well as the ability to restore one's identity. Weick cleverly calls this a kind of "vu ja de," or the opposite of "de ja vu." "I've never been here before, I have no idea where I am, and I have no idea who can help me" (Weick, 1993, pp. 634–635).

IDENTITY MAINTENANCE AS GOALODICY ON EVEREST

Weick's analysis of Mann Gulch as a cosmology episode provides a thoughtful contrast to the Everest climbers. If a cosmology episode entails a loss of identity in conjunction with the inability to restore one's identity, what occurred on Everest is the opposite. The teams continued to hold onto an identity even when that identity failed to serve the situation. The identity of the mountain climbers became tied so closely to the achievement of the goal that without the goal the team members could not recognize themselves. Abandoning the summit was akin to abandoning one's identity.

The ambitious and unquestionable pursuit of the summit became the dominant force behind participation on the team. It was the one thing that held the team together. Yet, the goal was a future state, an ideal rather than an actual identity. Stated in the form of a question, the identity went something like this: "How can I know who I am if I am not pursuing the summit?" Stated more generally, "How can I know who I am if I abandon my goal?" This question lies at the heart of goalodicy and provides another detail in the explanation for what happened on Everest.

WRITER'S BLOCK AT MANN GULCH vs. "REVERSE WRITER'S BLOCK" ON EVEREST

It helps to think of goalodicy as a kind of "reverse writer's block." Writer's block is a psychological condition that occurs to writers during the creative process. The term is frequently used to describe the inability to create new ideas or to put new words on a page. What happened at Mann Gulch can be considered a kind of writer's block. The teams lost the ability to come up with new ways to deal with the situation they faced.

In contrast, what happened on Everest constitutes just the opposite, a kind of reverse writer's block where a writer cannot stop writing, even after the book or other work has been completed. Putting this in terms of goal-setting, reverse writer's block occurs when a group continues to pursue a goal despite the fact that such pursuit no longer seems like a good idea. The Everest teams continued to climb because climbing was the only thing that made sense to them. Despite the growing lateness of the day and the impending storm, the teams ignored important information in narrow-minded pursuit of their goal. Like a writer unable to stop writing, despite the fact that she is out of good ideas, so the Everest teams continued to pursue the summit, despite the fact that, to paraphrase climber Ed Viesturs, they "should have turned around hours ago."

This "reverse writer's block"—failing to abandon a goal—can lead to disaster. Failure to revisit the prudence of goal pursuit can lead to a number of problems. Teams lean too heavily on prior learned experiences instead of developing new directions and skills that may be more appropriate under changing circumstances.

The breakdown of learning in teams

Learning breaks down on teams when three key factors come together (Kayes, 2004a):

1. A *narrowly defined goal*: attention is focused on achieving a clearly defined and specific outcome, such as "reaching the summit of Everest."
2. *Authoritative leadership*: team members depend so much on the leaders within the group that they cannot make decisions without involvement of the leader. For example, a leader determines when to abandon the summit of Everest for all or most of the team members.
3. *The emergence of complexity*: the environment contains multiple, often competing demands, and multiple possible goals begin to emerge. For example, during pursuit of the goal of reaching the summit of Everest, team leaders become separated from their team members, the ascent to the summit takes longer than expected, and the possibility of not getting back down alive suddenly must be taken into account along with reaching the summit.

Herein lies a recipe for what occurred on Everest. The combination of these three elements leads to the breakdown of learning in teams.

BREAKDOWN ON EVEREST

Learning broke down in the teams led by Fischer and Hall as the complexity faced by the team overcame their collective ability to manage the situation. Like a writer who cannot stop writing, the teams continued to pursue their goal despite the fact that it would soon lead to disaster. The teams continued for the summit, despite mounting evidence that the summit could not be safely attained. The breakdown of learning, just when learning was most required, emerged in seven steps.

First, highly motivated individual climbers sought to summit the world's highest peak. The challenge to accomplish more, to set and achieve new and higher goals, motivated the climbers to seek ever more exciting and prestigious peaks such as Everest. But beyond this generality, each of the climbers was probably motivated by different ultimate goals. Fischer and Hall were likely motivated by personal status, career success, and a more general enjoyment of leading and helping others reach challenging summits. Assistant guides were likely motivated by many of the same factors; some may have even wanted to get into the guide business themselves one day. Other guides, such as some of the Sherpa guides, while also seeking status among climbers, may have been motivated by money. Guiding hikes and climbs had become an important part of the Himalayan economy, and guiding has allowed the Sherpas to enjoy a high standard of living compared with other ethnic groups in Nepal. Despite the idealized view of Sherpa and Tibetan culture put forth by many, guiding on Everest and other Himalayan peaks provides an important source of income for many Sherpa villages. But even to suggest that an individual has only one goal, one desire, one purpose is to oversimplify things. Individuals are motivated by reaching multiple, even competing, goals.

Second, since few of the climbers had the individual resources to successfully summit of their own accord, they joined a team and acquired the benefits of shared resources. Even the most individual of efforts to summit Everest relied on support teams. For example, Reinhold Messner accomplished his "solo" effort to the summit of Everest without oxygen only with the help of other climbers and support teams. Lauded blind climber Erik Weihenmeyer achieved the summit of Everest only with the aid of a highly trained and able team of support staff to fix ropes and guides. Despite his experience and strength as a climber, Weihenmeyer would not have succeeded without the support of a strong team. The team provided the resources for a successful summit. The expenses of an expedition became manageable when the expedition costs were spread over 10 or 15 clients, each paying about $65,000. The cost of hiring a guide as well as several able-bodied assistants became more cost effective when the costs were spread over the team. Being part of a team meant that a person could now afford to hire the most successful and competent guides to help them to the top of the mountain.

Entering a team, however, brought with it several complications as well as benefits. Working together as a team meant competing goals. Individual goals began to compete with the team goal. But being part of a team also meant that people became interdependent. The individual actions of one person would impact the possible success of others. In addition, being part of a team created its own form of anxiety over working with others, especially when there are competing goals.

Third, team members fought for the limited attention of the team leaders. The need for the attention of the team leader created further complications as team members became dependent on the leaders for making decisions and taking actions. Dependence on leaders Fischer and Hall further reduced the ability of individual team members to make critical decisions on the mountain such as when to turn around and head back down. Without the presence of a leader to enforce the turn-around time, the individual members were left unable to make a decision and thus continued to pursue the summit with little concern for the impending storm or lateness of the day. A further complication emerged when Hall and Fischer decided to combine efforts and summit together. This "super team," made up of all the guides and clients, now totaled over 30 climbers. The super team created an even greater reliance on teamwork.

The combination of three events caused the situation to become more and more complicated with each passing hour. The guides became separated from their teams. The fact that the guides failed to fix ropes meant the time to reach the summit would take hours longer than originally planned. Because it would now take 14–16 hours instead of about 12 hours to reach the summit, the bottled oxygen supplies began to run out. Climbers became fatigued earlier in the climb. In addition, the large number of climbers on the mountain meant that each climber had only one chance to reach the summit.

When these three elements came together, the original goal of reaching the summit no longer worked. The team could no longer rely on the goal of reaching the summit to guide their action. Multiple goals emerged. The blinding storm, the failing team members all presented unforeseen problems not accounted for in the original goal of "standing on the top of the world." Team members could no longer rely on their leaders for direction. Hall was dedicating his efforts solely to the struggling client Doug Hansen, remembering that he had turned Hansen around just before the summit the year before.

The assistant leaders too stretched beyond capacity. Boukreev, who went without oxygen, decided to summit and return to high camp alone. His decision to pass by climbers meant that many clients were now on their own. Jangbu, one of Fischer's assistant guides, was now solely helping Pittman make it to the top. While a few guides remained with clients, they too were unable to make decisions. Beidleman was on the top of the summit for over an hour waiting for Fischer to give him the okay to descend. What had begun as a simple task, getting up the mountain, materialized into a complex and unquestionable nightmare for clients and guides.

None of these elements would matter alone. A narrow goal might be effective when the task is simple. Working together as a team might not prove important when the situation is predictable and calm. The fact that the groups became intermingled might not have mattered if decision-making authority had been built into the system. The fact that the team members remained dependent on their team leaders through most of the climb might not have mattered if the teams had not encountered the many complications. The leaders could have continued to make decisions all the way up the mountain like they had up to the final push to the summit. The fact that the teams encountered several problems on the final ascent should not, in and of itself, lead to disaster. A complicated problem can often be addressed quite effectively through learning. Leaders Hall and Fischer dealt effectively with setbacks throughout the climb. It was the combination of these items that led to the breakdown of learning. The combination of a narrow goal, authoritative leadership, and complications encountered during the climb led to disaster.

A look at this combination shows how these three ingredients worked together. The combination of things led to the breakdown of learning on Everest. What happened on Everest serves as the specific ingredients to develop a more general recipe for how learning breaks down during the pursuit of goals.

Recipe for a breakdown

The breakdown of learning on Everest can be described as a seven-stage process.

STEP 1: MOTIVATION TO ACHIEVE GOALS

First, individuals become motivated to achieve a goal. Motivation may emerge for a variety of reasons. The motivation may be to achieve fulfillment, social status, challenge, personal development, fame, or even the excitement and enjoyment of climbing itself. Ultimately, individuals set goals to achieve greater degrees of growth and development. Motivation starts the process.

STEP 2: NARROWLY DEFINED GOAL

The goal seeker defines the goal narrowly. The narrow definition of the goal is an attempt to simplify a complex process. Multiple goals really exist at one time, and the attempt to simplify leads to ignoring the dynamics of a multiple goal environment.

STEP 3: TEAM MEMBERSHIP AS A MEANS TO ACCOMPLISH THE GOAL

The goal seeker cannot accomplish the goal alone, so a team provides the force and resources needed. The complexity and community that naturally emerge from group dynamics require a new set of skills. What might be conceived of as an easy process when accomplished alone becomes more difficult when group processes become involved. If achieving a narrowly defined goal presents enough obstacles, then the team dynamic adds another layer of difficulty.

STEP 4: DEPENDENCE ON THE TEAM AND ESPECIALLY THE TEAM LEADER

The relationship between team members and team leaders can be challenging. Both team member and leader bring emotional demands and desires to the team that may not be clear. If the goal seeker lacks skill or confidence in his or her ability to accomplish the goal, then the goal seeker may become dependent on the leader. Dependence on the leader would emerge naturally, since the goal seeker entered the team for its resources anyway.

STEP 5: DECREASE IN THE EXERCISE OF AUTONOMY

Just as the situation begins to become more complex, the ability of the team members to deal with this complexity becomes constrained. More problems arise, but less problem solving takes place. The goal seeker becomes limited by his dependence on the leader. He becomes unable to make decisions, as he waits for the leader's intervention. He becomes blind to new information and remains focused on the narrowly defined goal. Instead of learning—remaining open to reciprocity of information— the goal seeker takes in and processes less information, and learning activity begins to break down.

STEP 6: INCREASE IN COMPLEXITY

Multiple conflicting goals emerge, making it too difficult for one leader to manage the complexity. In Step 6, the situation gets out of hand— or at least the situation gets out of the hands of the leaders. With this level of complexity, a higher level of leadership is required. In Step 6, learning and adaptation are required. Multiple goals begin to emerge, such that the original goal no longer seems robust enough. The original goal may split into multiple goals or may disappear altogether—either because it has already been achieved or because the situation demands a more complex way of thinking. One thing for sure, the leader can no longer manage the situation alone. He requires the input and help of other team members.

STEP 7: A BREAKDOWN OF LEARNING

A narrowly defined goal restricts learning, dependence on the leader further restricts learning, and complexity increases the need for learning. The simultaneous combination of these three elements means that learning breaks down exactly when it is needed the most. The demands of the situation require being open to new information and dynamic change, but the narrow focus of the goals restricts the amount of information going into the team. Further, the dependence of the team members on leaders restricts the ability of team members to respond to these changes. When the complexity increases, the team has yet to develop the ability to effectively respond to these new demands. Leadership cannot help now because the leader has become so overwhelmed that he or she too cannot possibly deal with everything.

The problem on Everest lied in the fact that the teams failed to function as learning teams until the leaders became severed from the group. Because of the changing environment and the unique demands of being an ad hoc team working on a one-time project, the teams required learning from the very start in order to achieve their goal. While team learning often emerges from internal sources—as when team members make a deliberate attempt to learn and develop—team learning can also be forced upon a team from outside circumstances. On Everest, the teams found themselves in an environment where learning became essential for survival. Learning was thrust upon the teams as they encountered various opportunities for learning.

Learning points

▶ A major problem with goalodicy lies in the fact that teams fail to learn because all efforts become focused on obtaining the goal. The single-minded pursuit of narrow goals leads to destructive goal pursuit.
▶ Goals become closely tied to identity, and sustained striving toward goals allows a team to maintain its current identity, even after that identity no longer proves real. This process was compared to "reverse writer's block," where a writer continues to write, despite not having anything valuable to write about.
▶ The breakdown of learning in teams as an attribute of goalodicy emerges when three factors intermingle: a narrowly defined goal, dependence on the leader, and the emergence of an ill-structured or complex problem.
▶ The emergence of goalodicy is described as a seven-step process, consisting of a motivation to achieve, a narrowly defined goal, team membership as a means to accomplish the goal, dependence on the team and especially the team leader, decrease in the exercise of autonomy, increase in complexity, and finally, as a result, a breakdown of learning.

Learning questions

▶ How did reaching the summit become the "identity" of the Everest teams? What evidence do you have for your response?
▶ What barriers to learning, in addition to goalodicy, did you see in the Everest disaster?

▶ Take another look at the seven-step process for the onset of goalodicy. At least in theory, breaking the pattern of goalodicy can occur at any stage of the process. What actions could the leaders or team members have taken to break the chain of events that led to goalodicy?

▶ Leaders may limit the autonomy and decision-making authority of individual team members. Can you think of other ways that team member autonomy and authority can be limited other than through authoritative leadership?

Part III   From Destructive to Productive Pursuit

7 Teamwork: Building the Foundation for Effective Goal Pursuit

The usual inhospitable weather patterns on Everest become unusually hospitable between May and June. This brief bit of relatively mild weather, sandwiched between the harsh winter and the summer monsoon, provides the window to the summit of Everest. The late morning this time of year can be particularly clear, almost pleasant. Since you are breathing the pure supplemental bottled oxygen, you feel a sense of euphoria and forget about the actual inhospitability of the environment. The afternoon sunshine lures you into complacency. The turnaround time that you planned on becomes easy to ignore. You forget that your visit to this inhospitable environment must be brief. It becomes hard to imagine an impending storm. You continue to pursue your goal of reaching the summit without abandon.

Slowly, irreversibly, the situation changes. The sun sets quickly in the mountains; dusk is surprisingly short. As the sun sets, the warm dry air that blessed the afternoon dissipates. The layer of moisture that coats the mountains quickly turns to fog and then to clouds and then to snow. Before you know it, the trail becomes engulfed in the white of a full-blown blizzard. The turnaround time that seemed almost trivial a few hours ago becomes exceedingly real.

But there is no time to think about turnaround times now. No time to think about the celebration at the top of the mountain, the pictures on the top of the world—or the weeks of climbing up and down to acclimatize, the months of preparation and conditioning, the years of dreaming. You'll attain the summit. But no one will greet you as victorious unless you make it back down.

You now find yourself without a leader, no one to tell you what to do or to validate your goal. Unlike the experienced climber who can fall back on years of experience on the mountain, you have only been in this situation a handful of times—and even then, you probably sat under the watchful eye of an experienced guide or mentor. If you are lucky, you might fall back on the authority of an assistant guide or a more experienced climber, but they too may be inexperienced in a leadership role despite their technical expertise. Organizing a diverse group is a different skill than reaching a narrowly defined goal.

Your body functions begin to slow. By now you have been awake for about 72 hours. You have taken an occasional catnap that is quickly interrupted by the sensation of suffocation. Lack of sleep marks only one of your problems. Your brain, like your lungs, is trying to compensate for the lack of oxygen. The high altitude sucks your body of water, and you have remained in a constant state of dehydration for days now. Even if you constantly drank, you could not replenish your body's fluids, and you can't carry enough water to adequately get back into shape. If you weren't too tired at camp the last 3 nights, you may have melted snow in your tent to rehydrate yourself, but that only amounted to a couple of liters when you need much more to simply survive. The dehydration affects your brain, and you carry with you what feels like a medium-grade hangover that further distracts you from the task of getting back down. The oxygen is essential for food digestion, so your body is starved for calories because you have had no appetite for the last few days or maybe even weeks. As a result, your blood sugar is low.

If you were thoughtful enough to buy an expensive pair of thermal boots, you are lucky because your toes are not yet numb. If you didn't buy these special boots, then it's possible that you can't feel your toes anymore. Either way, your boots have buckles rather than ties, and that's lucky because the blizzard prevents you from seeing the distance between your nose and your shoes to tie them. But then again, you couldn't take off your gloves to tie the shoes anyway because your figures would freeze in a matter of seconds. The wind chill is now negative 40 degrees Fahrenheit. Even your high-tech jacket can't keep you warm at that temperature, despite what the laboratory cold rating might say.

If you are like some climbers, under these conditions, you begin to panic and become irrational. You may reach into your Gore-Tex encased snowsuit and pull out your reserve energy booster and shoot yourself with a dose of adrenaline. The drug will restore your energy and help you think a little straighter, at least for a while.

Sleep deprivation, dehydration, hunger, blinding snow and cold, and limited brain functioning all conspire to distract you from the task at hand. Your individual capacity has been stretched beyond its limits. You and your leader are now separated by a healthy distance, and you begin to do the only thing you can: you turn to the most basic form of help. One thing that might get you out alive is something that you largely ignored from the beginning. You turn to those around you, the other members of your team for a way out together. Only when all your individual abilities have been exhausted will you turn to teamwork to get you through.

Up to this point, the book has largely taken for granted that the collection of climbers on Everest constituted a team. This chapter takes a more deliberate look at what constitutes a team and, more specifically, what factors lead to a successful team. The chapter begins by offering some definitions of teams and teamwork and argues that the collection of climbers on Mt Everest constituted a team. The chapter then builds a case for the importance of conversation as a source of teamwork. Conversation can lead to improved teamwork in several ways: it helps team members build interpersonal trust and understanding; it helps teams develop shared goals and coordinate their efforts; and it builds confidence among members that the goal can be reachable (Kayes, 2002b).

Everest expeditions as teamwork

EXPEDITIONS AS GROUPS

Analysis of events on Everest in 1996 has suggested that the assemblage of nearly 30 separate expeditions was representative of groups in organizations. The various coordinated activities of individuals on Everest met the basic definition of a group because the primary focus of decision-making, interaction, and communication was at the group level. The successful attainment of the goal required independent individuals acting together and using collective resources (Homans, 1950). Furthermore, these individuals came together for a specific purpose or task: climbing the mountain.

Kurt Lewin (1948), an early and highly influential thinker on group dynamics, contends that a team emerges when individuals share a common fate. Although many of the climbers under discussion here seemed to ignore their shared fate at first, the fact that the climbers needed each other to survive became clear in the final hours of the ordeal. Their future together would be tied to their common fate on the mountain. Lewin took the idea of shared fate among team members a step further. He claimed that a key characteristic of a team lies in that notion that members share goal interdependence. Goal interdependence exists when the actions of one individual have an impact on any or all other members of the group. One member's actions will impact the progress of another member in achieving the goal. In other words, the actions of one individual can either facilitate success or detract from success.

Scott Fischer seemed disturbed by the fact that Boukreev ascended to the summit without supplemental bottled oxygen. Boukreev's actions meant that he was unable to support climbers. That Fischer may have been so disturbed by Boukreev's decision to summit without oxygen and without helping clients indicates that he knew, at least intuitively, that Boukreev's actions would impact the team. Fischer might have also realized that his action in helping another climber down to safety just a few days before the final summit might have impacted his team negatively because he would become weakened by the 8-hour ordeal.

Krakauer and others reacted with disdain and puzzlement when they noticed Fischer's assistant guide Jangbu short-roping Pittman up the mountain on the final ascent. They seemed to know that this action could impede their own summit attempt. These and other thoughts by climbers suggest that climbers knew that each group member's fate was linked and that achieving the summit required working together as a team. The actions of one person could impact the ability of another to accomplish the goal. This interdependence provides the basic ingredient for a team. The distinction between a group and a team, however, is a foggy one, so the criteria for what constitutes a team deserve some additional attention.

EXPEDITIONS AS TEAMS

One observer of group behavior suggests an unsettling metaphor to understand the distinction between a group and a team. Imagine a group of people who fly as passengers on a plane to a common destination. This is a group of people since they share a goal of getting to the same location, but they are not a team because the action of any one person is unlikely to impact the outcome of arriving at the destination safely. The passengers share a common desired outcome, but not the means to help or hinder achieving that outcome. The relationships change, however, if the plane is hijacked by a group of passengers (see Brown, 2000, p. 35). Then the passengers become a team as they act together toward a new goal and their interdependence becomes established.

The hijacking metaphor may be instructive about the distinction between a group and team, yet its distinctions are too restrictive. In fact, the action of one passenger always carries the possibility of impacting the actions of other passengers. It is not simply that a team exists when a person's actions *actually* impact the outcome of a goal; instead, a team exists any time a person has the *potential* to have that impact. The metaphor implies that individuals fail to recognize this possibility. This was true on Everest: the team members failed to explicitly recognize their interdependence as a group until a dramatic set of events unfolded and they had no choice but to see themselves as a team.

Even though the Everest climbers failed to explicitly recognize themselves as a team, the elements of teamwork were at play from the start of the expedition. The climbers on the mountain met the minimum definition of a team from the very beginning because they shared responsibility and interdependence for getting to the summit. The actions of each individual had the potential to facilitate or hinder the chances of every other member.

TEAMS IN ACTION

The Everest groups constituted an action team (Sundstrom, DeMeuse, and Futrell, 1990, p. 120). According to Eric Sundstrom, a well-known team researcher and consultant, action teams "confront sudden, unpredictable behavior... that demands quick and sometimes impro-vised responses." One of the specific characteristics of an action team is that individuals have specialized skills that contribute to the success of the team. These skills enable the action team to function at a higher level than individual members would function. Sundstrom believes that one of the most important aspects of success for action teams lies in the coordination of these special skills. Coordination consists of three elements:

1. *Special skill sets.* On Everest, all members had to have specialized climbing abilities, such as knowing how to use ropes, harnesses, and other equipment. Climbing also requires expert judgment, such as how to navigate difficult terrain.
2. *Synchronization of skills among team members.* On Everest, team members needed to coordinate skills such as setting ropes, agreeing on a summit schedule, and aiding weaker climbers.
3. *Mutual adjustment to individual members.* Climbing Everest required that individual team members adjust to individual team members' personalities. For example, according to some accounts, Scott Fischer became disillusioned with his assistant guide Anatoli Boukreev, who decided to summit alone without bottled oxygen. But Fischer seem-ingly adapted to Boukreev's style by allowing him to pursue the summit under those terms anyway.

Another element related to action teams is that they often depend on a high degree of external support for their success. This was the case on Everest too, where team members relied on the nearly 400 staff members to supply and support the 30 or so expeditions on Everest in 1996. Action teams also require access to timely and explicit information. As one group of researchers observed,

Information needs of action teams reflect the intense, dynamic, high-stakes, time-critical, and externally driven nature of their work. [Action teams] must respond, often with little notice, to challenging and rapidly changing events and conditions generated for example by formidable adversaries, unfavorable environments, and watchful stakeholders. (Bikson, Cohen, and Mankin, 1999, p. 230)

The first successful summit of Everest, which included team members Hillary and Norgay, illustrates the nature of an action team, how it depends on its environment, and most importantly how it organizes various types of work. All successful expeditions in the Himalayas require the support of Sherpas. The term *Sherpa*, which translate as "people from the East" denotes the particular culture of people that have become the lifeblood of expeditions. Christoph Von Furer-Haimendorf (1984), an anthropologist provided some of the first systematic documentation of the Sherpa culture. He observed the Sherpa culture for over 30 years. He describes the importance of Sherpas, especially the head Sherpa called a "Sidar" in organizing the complexities of an Everest expedition.

An important role in the organization of expedition labor has always been played by the *sidar*, men of exceptional ability to control and lead other porters. Such foremen, once engaged by a group of mountaineers usually insist on being entrusted with the recruiting of the other Sherpas. By doing so they build up a position of influence and economic power. (p. 65)

Sherpas play an important part in each of the four types of teams that were involved in the 1953 expedition. First, ferry or carrying Sherpa teams brought fuel, food, and other supplies to the camps at different heights. The carrying teams ensured that the expedition received the necessary support during the campaign. Second, Sherpa support teams worked to make each camp as efficient as possible. They cooked, washed, and completed other duties necessary to support the daily operations of the expedition. Third, Sherpa climbing teams helped set ropes and break trails or followed assault teams to establish camps. Finally, the assault teams, which almost always require the support of Sherpas, helped in the push for the summit.

The first successful summit included several assault teams. Each assault team essentially competed with the other teams for the opportunity to push higher. Hillary and Norgay represented only one of several assault teams and may have been chosen to push for the summit only after another assault team failed in their early push. The various types of teams, each serving a unique function, became an essential part of the first successful summit.

Action teams, like those who climb Everest, provide a unique setting to explore the nature of teamwork. Indeed, not all teams face the dynamic conditions or the highly consequential outcomes these teams face. In less dynamic environments, such as on shop floors or in business organizations, poor teamwork can go unnoticed because consequences of team failure are not so dramatic. When consequences for team failure are less visible, teamwork can be avoided in favor of individual efforts or lower outputs. Yet, despite these differences, important lessons can be drawn from action teams.

TASK FORCES

One specific way that action teams, like those on Everest, can serve as guides to teamwork more generally can be found in the task force, a common form of team found in nearly all organizations. Members of task forces have at least four characteristics. They:

▶ have different specialties suited to perform the task and do not normally work closely together
▶ exercise decision autonomy and environmental dependence
▶ create a single act or performance event
▶ are constrained by specific time deadlines (Hackman, 1990, p. xviii).

Task forces usually consist of team members with diverse backgrounds who come together to make a decision or recommendation or to solve a specific problem. A task force in a hospital, for example, may come together to improve patient care or reduce errors. In a manufacturing environment, a task force may carry responsibility for improving safety or increasing production output. In service organizations, task forces often serve as the core of decision-making for the organization. For example, in an accounting firm, a team of diverse audit specialists may come together to conduct an audit during tax season. In a management consulting firm, a group of consultants may come together to assess and make recommendations for improving an organization's strategic direction. Whatever the nature of the team and its task, all teams function because individual members share knowledge in the effort to achieve a desired state. Members share this knowledge by engaging in conversation.

Conversation in teams

Conversation plays an important role in teamwork because it serves as the source of communication and learning. Conversation describes the process of interpreting and understanding human experience through language (Baker, Jensen, and Kolb, 2002). In conversation, knowledge moves from being individual, trapped inside the experience of an individual team member, to being a social process. Conversation serves as the medium for teams to get things done. The importance of conversation in the process of teamwork cannot be overstated. Without engaged conversation, teamwork fails to exist.

Conversation plays an important part in all teams, but in mountain climbing, talk can be the difference between life and death. A closer look at the importance of conversation in mountain-climbing activities helps illuminate its importance in teams more generally. Conversation comes into play in mountain climbing in at least three important ways: coordinating, debriefing, and storytelling.

COORDINATING

First, conversation enables the coordination of specific actions between climbers. Rope commands provide a specific example. Climbers who are roped together during a climb are interdependent and must communicate every action to ensure that climbing partners understand their actions and intentions. Rope commands give instructions, commands, or information necessary for each action, even each step. For example, a climber might yell to his partner "belay on" to indicate that he has put tension on the rope so the other member can ascend up a short stretch aided by the tension of the rope. Then the second climber would respond "belay on" to confirm the command of the first climber (Mitchell, 1983, p. 70).

DEBRIEFING

Debriefing serves as another type of conversation. During a debriefing session, teams collect, disseminate, and apply newly learned knowledge. Debriefing serves several important team functions. The importance of debriefing for teams became apparent when Micha Popper and Raanan Lipshitz (1998) studied transcripts of the Israeli Defense Force/Air Force. Specifically, they looked at the after-action review sessions conducted by teams of pilots just after they had returned from flight-training sessions (see Marinko, 1991). They describe the nature of these sessions. Each cockpit is equipped with a video camera that records the day's flight, similar to the "black box" found in commercial airlines but with the addition of video. Each team of pilots, composed of either two or four members, debriefs the clip, taking close notes on every action taken in the cockpit but with special emphasis on incidents that could be seen as mistakes or important actions. These special incidents are then taken to another debriefing session, where they are rehashed with the entire squadron (Marinko, 1991, pp. 167–168).

The researchers found that the highly trained action teams spent between 40 and 50 percent of operational time in debriefing. This means that debriefing was as much a part of effective teamwork as the action itself. Debriefing, they concluded, served at least three purposes in teamwork.

1. *Social control*: Debriefing allows team members to monitor the performance of other team members. It forces team members to come up with a plausible explanation for errors and thus serves as a kind of disciplining mechanism as well.
2. *Psychological safety*: Debriefing builds resilience within the team so that members can be forthright and direct with one another. This intensity leads to bonding among team members through involvement and recognition of the contributions of others.
3. *Learning*: Debriefing allows team members to use their experiences to make judgments, adjust perceptions, and improve outcomes.

STORYTELLING

Debriefing improves teamwork because it creates a structural mechanism to help teams by setting aside specific time for review. Conversation also serves another purpose in teamwork: it serves as the medium for storytelling. Mountain climbers are passionate about storytelling. The stories of their successes and defeats provide the basis for much of what is known about the efforts of mountain climbing and the thoughts of mountain climbers. Mountain climbers then avidly read these books. Reading fills the boredom brought about by long lulls between climbing and resting or waiting out storms.

These stories serve a purpose in the mountain-climbing community. Stories serve as lessons for action. Stories provide a form of identity about what it takes to be among the best climbers. Stories guide behavior by providing details of what action to take under different conditions. Stories set the boundaries of culture by showing who is part of the climbing community and who is not.

Stories from past climbs alert climbers to possible mistakes or mishaps. Climbers share stories like that of Marty Hoey, the first American woman to attempt Everest. In 1982, Hoey fell to her death on a relatively simple yet icy and steep part of the climb, just 1500 feet below the summit. When Hoey stepped back away from a rope to allow a fellow to take off his pack, she suddenly started sliding down the mountain and eventually fell off a cliff to her death. The fact that Hoey's climbing harness remained attached to the rope meant that she failed to properly secure the harness to her body. The Hoey story proves that even an experienced and attentive climber can make unwitting mistakes on the mountain.

Hoey's tragic story of not properly clipping in should have been a warning to another climber on the 1996 Taiwanese team. On the morning before the final assault for the summit, Chen Yu-nan emerged from his tent not wearing his boots, not his ice-clinging crampons but the smooth insulating boot liners. When the slippery material hit the frictionless ice, Chen lost his footing and slid a few hundred yards down the mountain. Chen was forced to abandon his summit bid. Fischer spent the day short-roping Chen down the mountain where Chen eventually died.

The direction the story takes serves as an important lesson. Yiannis Gabriel (2004), an innovative thinker on management and organizations, suggests that stories consist of themes, plots, characters, motives, adventures, and predicaments. Stories provide memorable ways to recount prior actions which, importantly, serve as a guide for future action. Stories preserve. Stories direct. Stories provide a form of authority for what is appropriate for action.

An important part of storytelling is its reliance on specialized language, which allows climbers to communicate climbing-specific jargon. The role that specialized language plays is both technical and social. In a technical function, specialized language allows individuals to communicate quickly and easily with shared language, avoiding excess words. For example, by saying "you need crampon" rather than "you need the spikes that clip on the bottom of boots that allow you to climb on ice because this section of the climb contains ice," a leader can communicate a much more complex demand with much fewer words.

In addition to its technical purpose, specialized language serves a social purpose. By demonstrating knowledge of technical language, a person communicates that he or she is a part of the mountain-climbing community. Language, along with dress and specific tools, provides one of the most powerful indicators of a culture. People can always recognize that they encounter a new culture when they hear a highly technical language (Mitchell, 1983).

A story that might serve as a good lesson for mountain climbers can be seen in the movie *The Mountain*. Spencer Tracy plays an experienced mountain climber who climbs primarily for the joy and thrill of the sport. Tracy plays opposite a young Robert Wagner. Wagner can be described as a materialistic goal seeker. He wants to loot a wrecked plane but knows he cannot reach the plane without Tracy's experience. Wagner tells Tracy that the climb will be spectacular, unlike any he has done before. Tracy, against his better judgment, takes Wagner's bait. During the climb, however, Wagner continues to push for the summit and the loot, while Tracy, overwhelmed by the experience itself, loses sight of the goal. Wagner's concentration on the goal is offset by Tracy's concentration on the process. Wagner's expertise in climbing in difficult weather is complemented by Tracy's experience on various peaks. This fictional account of climbing illustrates how two individuals with different experiences draw on each other's strengths to reach the summit.

Although this Hollywood movie targets a more general audience than mountain climbers, the story illustrates something important about climbing. The movie has all the elements of a good story. The story involves interesting characters facing a series of dilemmas and challenges. The way this two-person team, composed of Tracy and Wagner, confronts and eventually resolves the dilemma makes for interesting viewing. Stories like these form the basis of teamwork as teams develop stories about their feats and draw on the experience of members in conversation.

Team shared beliefs

One way conversation works in teams is by facilitating shared beliefs among team members. Shared beliefs describe the way the group thinks about itself. Shared beliefs are similar to norms, the psychological structures that develop in groups. Like shared beliefs, norms constitute the kinds of beliefs that come to be expected by members of the group. Shared beliefs come to constitute what is considered normal behavior in the group. Shared beliefs serve several purposes. They:

▶ set limits of acceptable or unacceptable behavior
▶ create predictable environments and set expectations for members
▶ facilitate the achievement of group goals (as opposed to purely individual goals)
▶ form a common identity and determine the boundaries of out-group members (Brown, 2000, p. 64).

Shared beliefs constitute another basis for a team. When team members share beliefs, teamwork can begin to take place.

The nature of a shared belief may facilitate or inhibit a team as it works toward its goals. Certain shared beliefs foster good teamwork and goal achievement. Other beliefs, however, prevent teams from achieving their desired outcomes.

The negative effects of certain shared beliefs on goal achievement can be seen on Everest. It seems that the shared belief of achieving a narrow goal led to the problems. One observer made sense of the unacceptable death rates on Everest in 1996 and 1997 in the *British Medical Journal.* He wrote:

> The most striking factor is the developing narrow mindedness of some climbers. During the preparations back home the climbers get more and more engaged in their expeditions. Family and friends get less attention as the day of departure approaches. Then they move to a remote and isolated area concentrating only on one single objective—reaching the summit. If they meet other people, these are fellow climbers with the same goals, undergoing the same psychological changes. Their appearances may confirm the normality of the climbers' absurd behavior, and a typical subculture is formed. The perspective of life may change, and some climbers become obsessed by their task. High on the mountain, the only things that matter are reaching the summit, keeping warm, and having enough oxygen. During such a mental challenge climbers may avoid helping each other, they do not see descent as an alternative, they push to summit too late, and eventually they die. (Rostrup, 1998, p. 81)

This thought-provoking comment describes how certain shared beliefs can lead to negative consequences. The shared belief in the narrow goal of getting to the summit limited the perspective of the team. Goalodicy, one negative shared belief, is discussed in detail in this book; here, attention is focused on some positive shared beliefs. Since the 1950s and possibly earlier, scholars have focused on two types of shared beliefs that can improve teamwork: beliefs related to interpersonal processes and beliefs about task processes. Each is discussed in turn.

INTERPERSONAL BELIEFS: INTERPERSONAL UNDERSTANDING AND INTERPERSONAL TRUST

Interpersonal beliefs focus on the social dimensions of groups, such as how members perceive and feel about one another or how much they can empathize with the other members. These beliefs are often called maintenance beliefs because they maintain the spirits of the group. Over years of research and thousands of studies on team dynamics, researchers have identified a host of interpersonal processes related to positive team outcomes. Two of these shared beliefs, however, have gained much attention in recent years: interpersonal understanding and interpersonal trust.

Interpersonal understanding describes the degree to which team members can recognize and comprehend the emotional states, preferences, skills, or relationships of individuals in the group (Druskat and Kayes, 1999, 2000). Although interpersonal understanding has long been associated with positive team outcomes, researchers have shown a renewed interest in interpersonal understanding because it is related to emotional intelligence. Emotional intelligence is the process whereby individuals develop self-awareness, self-control, or the ability to self-monitor, and the ability to understand and influence others. A key ability of emotional intelligence is monitoring others' emotions and moods.

Druskat and Wolff (2001) have suggested that group emotional intelligence, and in particular interpersonal understanding, is an important component of team effectiveness. They argue that group emotional intelligence leads to trust, identity, and efficacy, which in turn lead to participation, cooperation, and collaboration and then to better decisions, more creative solutions, and higher productivity. In groups that display high degrees of interpersonal understanding, members express the following:

▶ Knowing the thoughts, feelings, or moods of other team members
▶ Understanding the particular issues being faced by team members
▶ Knowing the attitudes and views of other team members.

Interpersonal trust describes the shared belief among team members that the team is safe for interpersonal risk taking. Interpersonal trust describes the tacit or taken-for-granted assumption that it is okay to take risks and express dissenting opinions in the team. A number of theorists have called this process *psychological safety* (Edmondson, 1999, p. 354). Like the team belief of interpersonal understanding, the concept of psychological safety has been around for a long time. Abraham Maslow (1998), the well-known humanist psychologist, considered psychological safety essential for human growth and development. Maslow believed that individuals needed an environment high in psychological safety in order to grow and develop.

Trust helps ensure that all voices in the team are heard and respected without undue influence from a few individuals. Also, trust helps to manage peer pressure and limit certain problems that occur when groups become too focused on a single and limited course of action. In groups with high degrees of interpersonal trust, team members feel comfortable:

▶ telling other members about mistakes
▶ expressing ideas that are different from those of other group members or expressing multiple points of views

▶ dealing with conflict
▶ challenging the dominant point of view, whether that point of view is
  related to a powerful person such as a leader or is the dominant view of
  the group.

These four elements of interpersonal trust help expose and manage power
dynamics in the team so that one dominant member, such as a formal or
informal leader, does not monopolize the team.

TASK BELIEFS: GOAL SHARING AND TEAM EFFICACY

Task-related beliefs are another form of shared beliefs. When team members
share these beliefs relative to the task, they may be more effective in achieving
their goal. Teams with shared task-related beliefs share the same goal.
Members may know the specific goals of individual team members, especially if they differ from the team's general goal, but the focus is on the team's
goal and the team's success rather than the goals or success of a specific
individual.
    All members know the purpose of the team. There is an important
distinction between having an individual goal and a shared group goal. For
example, each of the individuals on the summit teams had a goal of reaching
the summit. On the other hand, the team members shared no sense of a
team goal. The difference between an individual and team goal is that an
individual goal can be accomplished without the help of or involvement in a
team. As Mills (1967) stated with a team goal, "the way to reach one's individual goal is through working with others in order to accomplish the group
goal . . . accomplishing a group goal is a means toward individual goals"
(p. 83). Team goal sharing, as apposed to common individual goals within
the same team, becomes evident when team members demonstrate the
following:

▶ viewing the team as the means to achieve a personal goal
▶ sharing a team goal with other team members
▶ focusing activity on meeting team goals rather than individual goals
▶ achieving team success rather than just individual success
▶ sharing a common purpose as a team.

    Efficacy is the shared belief among team members that their team can
accomplish a task or complete a project better than other groups to which it
will be compared. While research on team efficacy has produced mixed findings, there is a strong belief that efficacy is an important part of effective team
functioning. A more recent conceptualization and review of the research

suggests that team efficacy is important only to a point, but it can also have detrimental effects. A team must be confident enough to feel that it can be effective, but it must also be humble enough to realize where it needs to improve or change. Efficacy presents a form of paradox.

Thomas Nelson, a researcher with some climbing experience as well, wrote in his climbing journal about how events can impact one's confidence. He recounted the experience after his return to Seattle:

> One day while climbing, [Nelson] felt too warm and decided to remove his pile vest. He stopped, took off his pack and then his windbreaker, had a drink of water from the water bottle in his pack, put the windbreaker and pack on again, and continued to climb; several hundred feet later, he still felt too hot and decided to remove his windbreaker, stopped, took off his pack, and upon taking off his windbreaker, was shocked to discover that he had never removed his pile vest at the earlier stop! (Nelson *et al.*, 1990, p. 372)

Nelson's experience happened during a research study he led on Everest in 1988. The study on high altitude sheds light on the nature of the efficacy paradox. Nelson and the team of researchers sought to identify if the effects of high altitude, namely oxygen deprivation, impaired learning. They presented climbers with a number of different scenarios at the relatively low altitude of Katmandu (1200 m), again at base camp (5400 m), Camp II (6500 m), and Camp III (7100 m), and then again in Katmandu after returning from the summit attempt. The first round of experiments measured the effects of altitude on the simple recall of facts. The climbers then went through several more rounds of experiments. In the follow-up rounds, the experimenter only presented questions that the climber got wrong on the first round of questions. The second set of rounds determined how confident a climber would be in getting the answer to the questions correct if the climber had access to a list of possible choices. The second round of experiments was designed to measure the climber's confidence in his or her problem solving ability. The experimenters called this confidence a "feeling of knowing."

The researchers found no significant difference in knowledge recall among climbers based on altitude; recall remained about the same across different altitudes. What researchers did find was more remarkable. Researchers found that confidence in the ability to solve problems, the feeling of knowing, was significantly stronger at lower altitudes than at higher altitudes. In other words, as climbers went higher up the mountain, their confidence in their own ability to solve problems decreased.

The researchers concluded that climbers' confidence in their ability to recall important information during a climb became impaired. They concluded that altitude has a particularly harsh effect on problem-solving ability, not necessarily on information recall. Indeed, effects of altitude may have played a part in limiting brain and body functioning. The researchers point to another explanation, however, that is more intriguing. The alternative explanation is based on the psychology of climbing as well as the nature of efficacy and learning. The researchers suggested that climbers increasingly accept the risks they face as they ascend up the mountain.

Confidence, or efficacy, in the belief that they can adequately solve problems drops as the summit nears. Essentially, climbers become more pessimistic the closer they get. The researchers quote the well-known high-altitude climber Chris Bonington to illustrate the point. Bonington wrote: "The isolation and constant stress of risk we had been under in the last few days deadened my reaction further. It wasn't callousness, rather the acceptance of the inherent risk we constantly lived under" (cited in Nelson *et al.*, 1990, p. 372).

Surely, Nelson and his associates point out, the realities of mountain climbing can account for only a portion of the lower sense of efficacy as climbers approach the summit; the physical effects of altitude must also play a part. Yet, the psychological efficacy and its role in helping teams successfully achieve goals need to be taken seriously, regardless of the effects of altitude. Indeed, the research of Nelson and the experience of other climbers might suggest a trade-off to be achieved between too much confidence and too little confidence. Climbers need enough confidence to believe they are capable of getting to the summit. At the same time, they must recognize their own limitations. Too much confidence could contribute to the destructive pursuit of goals; too little confidence could contribute to cowering from pursuit of goals. One approach may be for teams to gauge their level of efficacy and determine for themselves what level is needed for success. Teams can gauge efficacy by:

▶ seeing themselves as capable of achieving a goal relative to other teams with the same resources
▶ believing they are capable of achieving their goal
▶ possessing confidence in their ability as a team.

Higher team functioning

The shared beliefs of interpersonal understanding, trust, goal sharing, and efficacy serve as the basis for effective teamwork. For the benefits of teamwork to emerge, teams need to develop and to strive to function at a higher level than a group of individuals working independently. This higher group functioning, as it is sometimes called, emerges when certain key group dynamics have been achieved. Several signs point to higher functioning:

▶ Team members are accepting individual differences.
▶ Conflict on the team is reserved for the task rather than emotional issues.
▶ The team's purpose and goals are decided through rational discussion rather than an attempt at unanimity.
▶ Members are aware of the various emotional issues that exist in the group but have arrived at a comfortable level of conflict.
▶ Members have a greater awareness of others' individual expectations and goals (adapted from Bennis and Shepard, 1956).

A high-functioning group emerges when members can adapt to new circumstances and learn to deal with the inevitable conflicts and challenges inherent in pursuing a collective goal. Ultimately, whether or not a team will achieve a higher level of functioning depends on a team's ability to learn. The next chapter explores the process of team learning.

Learning points

▶ The Everest expedition efforts can be described in terms of groups, teams in action, and task forces. Characteristics of teamwork include the sharing of a common fate, the sharing of a common goal, and interdependence in terms of tasks and outcomes.
▶ Conversation plays an important part in understanding teamwork. The process of mountain climbing helps to illustrate some of the functional roles of conversations in teams, including coordination of activities and thoughts, specialized language, debriefing, and storytelling.
▶ Shared beliefs are one important defining characteristic of a team. A few shared beliefs are important for functional goal-setting. Interpersonal beliefs include understanding of other team members and trust. Task beliefs include shared goals. Efficacy, or confidence, has had mixed effects.
▶ Ultimately, for a group to function well at complex tasks, it must first establish shared beliefs among team members that lead to good teamwork. Once these have been established, a team can begin to learn its way to achieving goals.

Learning questions

▶ What kinds of shared beliefs were in operation among the Everest groups? Which of these beliefs, in your view, led to effective or ineffective team-work?

▶ How did the leaders of these teams foster these shared beliefs you iden-tified?

▶ Think of a team you have been on in the past 6 months. What was effective about that team and what was ineffective? How did this team meet the definition of teamwork described in this chapter? Are there other factors that define a team not mentioned here?

▶ Return to the elements of good teamwork described in this chapter. Which shared beliefs did you experience in your team? Interpersonal understanding and trust? Shared goals? Efficacy?

8 Team Learning: Responding to Organizational and Environmental Complexity

You are trapped. You made it to the top of the world's highest mountain, but now you struggle with your teammates to get down. You are caught in a blinding storm and your body is about to give out. Even though you are only a few hundred yards from a safe camp, with tents and oxygen, you cannot navigate through the blinding storm that engulfs you. You begin to rely heavily on your teammates—members of other teams, who were once your competition, may be your only chance to survive. You try to talk to team members but soon realize the difficulties of communicating in a blinding storm. The wind, snow, and craziness of the situation make verbal communication almost impossible. You try hand signals but those too are difficult to see in the blinding snow. Normal modes of communication have broken down.

You depend on your teammates and your teammates depend on you. You have trained for weeks together and you know your teammates well. You avoided working with them in many instances and you really don't like many of them, but you still know how they act. Since you cannot communicate well, you try everything you can to coordinate your activities with teammates. You begin to anticipate how other teammates might act. You size up who is in good enough shape to depend on and who is not. You size up who can move and who can't, what each member might contribute to your team, who will know the way out and who will drag you down. You assess your own state of mind and your mind's resources. The bottled oxygen ran out hours ago and you are on your own. You only planned to be up here for 17 hours or so. Your oxygen was designed to last for 16 hours, but now you sit on the edge of 17.

You begin to coordinate with your team members, but since you cannot communicate clearly you coordinate by anticipating each other's actions and thoughts. You imagine the struggle and you anticipate their actions. You know that some people are looking for breaks in the clouds, perhaps to spot a star to find the direction of camp. You take turns pounding your teammates to keep them awake. The pounding keeps the blood moving— whatever blood hasn't already frozen. Without thinking too much about it, you are working as a team. Your teammates do the same. You check periodically, when you can, to see if they continue to act in their own way. All the while, you know your teammates are keeping the team alive, even though you do not know exactly how. Suddenly, irreversibly, you share the goal of getting back alive.

This chapter begins by looking at how the Everest teams learned to get back alive by taking advantage of opportunities for learning during the descent. The emphasis is on the fact that in many cases teamwork is not enough. Teams must shift from teamwork to team learning. The chapter argues that it was ultimately this shift from teamwork to team learning that led to the eventual survival of teams on Everest. Moving from the concrete description of the events to the abstract ideas of analysis, the chapter describes the general process of learning. A simplified model of learning is presented and explained in terms of the events.

The chapter concludes by explaining how team learning leads to the development of a higher level of team functioning through a complex goal structure. The final section outlines a five-phase process for developing this complex goal structure in teams. A better understanding of how goals develop in teams underscores how teams, like those on Everest, must respond to more complex situations with more complex goal-setting processes. Teams working in a complex and changing environment must continually update goals in response to changing internal and external demands. In a dynamic environment, learning and not simply goal pursuit becomes the primary task of teams.

Taking advantage of opportunities for learning

If a team that works wants to transform into a team that learns, it must take advantage of opportunities for learning. Opportunities for learning emerge when teams find themselves in novel situations, as when members experience a discrepancy between what they expect to happen and what actually happens.

Scott Fischer's assistant guide Neil Beidleman experienced such a discrepancy when he found himself on top of the mountain with clients, waiting for Fischer to arrive to give him the go ahead to descend. Beidleman expected Fischer to be there with him much earlier, but Fischer was trailing behind with slower climbers. Beidleman did not expect to have to wait for an hour and a half, an unusually long and even dangerous amount of time on the summit.

In addition to this discrepancy between expectation and reality, Beidleman had an opportunity for learning because of the gap between the task at hand (leading a group down the mountain) and his skill (sole leadership ability to get the team down). Even though Beidleman had prior experience in expeditions, the year 1996 was different because of the larger number of relatively inexperienced climbers and the logistical challenges involved in having over 300 total climbers on the mountain. When Beidleman joined with Mike Groom, Rob Hall's assistant guide, to lead these climbers down the mountain, the two assistant guides found themselves sharing a leadership role, and this too presented an opportunity for learning, since the two assistants were not only new at being the leaders, they were also new at sharing leadership.

It is not likely that Beidleman had expected to be the sole leader, nor is it likely that he had all the information necessary to get down the mountain safely. Just as he had decided to stay on the summit and wait for Fischer before descending, Beidleman needed additional information before he could effectively do his job. Beidleman sought information about when to leave from Fischer. Beidleman shows how an opportunity for learning occurs when people actively seek new information in their environment.

Another opportunity for learning occurred when the new leaders found themselves trapped in a snowstorm with no clear direction to the safety of camp. The two tried different things to get down the mountain. The various attempts at getting back to camp safely from the huddle show how difficult it is to learn from experience.

Team learning

Opportunities for team learning occur because individuals put themselves in a position in which their current knowledge is pushed to the limit. Learning means more than simply developing new ways to accomplish a task (see Seijts and Latham, 2005). Learning involves a number of different processes related to the acquisition and transformation of knowledge (Kolb, 1984). As a process of knowledge creation, team learning describes a process of constant exploration and adjustment. For example, team learning involves a "combination of reciprocity to new information with a readiness to revise past assessments of a situation" (Mills, 1967, p. 98). Learning requires moving from the all-knowing team and team leader to a mode of humility, recognizing what the team and team leader do not yet know. In practice, being able to understand what is not yet known requires selecting and screening information so that everyone in the team can distinguish between what is important and what is irrelevant to the situation at hand. Learning in teams involves a number of interrelated processes:

▶ recognizing discrepancies between the team's available resources and the resources that are needed
▶ adapting to new situations by engaging directly with the environment
▶ using information to solve problems
▶ creating new knowledge in response to changing demands
▶ drawing on experience to make judgments and inform action.

Learning vs. performance

Understanding why learning plays such an important role in successful goal achievement helps to clearly distinguish between learning and performance. Teams often focus on performance goals like getting to the top of the mountain. This focus on achieving a clear but narrow goal encourages performance-directed behaviors. When teams are dominated by performance-driven behaviors, they begin to ignore the new challenges that might emerge. These new challenges are likely to emerge when problems are ill-defined. Table 3 describes some of the differences between learning and performance processes that emerge during goal pursuit.

In reality, achieving most goals requires both learning- and performance-directed behaviors. However, as the Everest incident illustrates, performance-directed behaviors often emerge at the expense of learning behaviors. A single-minded drive to put one foot in front of the other may mark the path to successful goal achievement, but not watching your step can lead to disaster.

One of the problems that led to death on Everest was the fact that the leaders thought they had the work processes all figured out. Fischer

Table 3 **Process considerations for learning vs. performance**

Process consideration	Performance	Learning
Nature of problem solving	Improve old strategies	Generate new strategies
Nature of goals	Single goal	Multiple goals
Nature of work processes	Established	Difficult to maintain
Complexity of goal	Low	High
Reliance on prior strategies	High	Low
Need for adaptability	Low	High
Definition of goals	Narrow	Broad

had been known to say, "These days, I'm telling you, we've built a yellow brick road to the summit." Yet in reality, many details of climbing Everest had not been figured out. The unknowns existed because the leaders failed to account for certain contingencies, like the separation of the team members from the leaders, the longer-than-expected time to ascend, and the complexity of the group dynamics during the final push to the summit.

Over the many years of climbing on Everest, Everest teams have developed knowledge about how to summit successfully. Climbers develop certain rules of the game. These rules include what time of the year to summit. Most expeditions summit during a short window of time in May. Reaching the summit should occur no later than 2:00 p.m. in the afternoon to allow for time to get down safely. Fixed ropes speed ascent and descent. All of these insights, gathered over the course of the history of mountain climbing, add up to the knowledge of climbing Everest. Climbers learned these rules informally, through the collective experience of the mountain-climbing community.

The process of learning

Just because a person comes into contact with an opportunity for learning does not mean he or she will learn. Learning requires the person to go beyond the immediate experience, reflect upon it, and take action. David Kolb (1984), a professor of organizational behavior, introduced a four-stage model of learning nearly 30 years ago. Today, Kolb's model is one of the most influential models of learning and development. His model and subsequent research on how people learn from experience has inspired thousands of studies and papers. According to Kolb, learning involves four interrelated stages:

1. *Concrete experience:* feelings, emotions, and direct experience with the world. This stage involves generating new experiences and ideas that serve as the basis for learning.
2. *Reflective observation:* looking back on an initial experience and gathering new information and ideas about the experience. This stage requires looking at experience from different viewpoints, reflecting, and gathering new data to make sense of the experience.
3. *Abstract conceptualization:* organizing the initial experience into a coherent and meaningful context. This stage requires abstract thinking that creates a plan to guide future actions.
4. *Active experimentation:* testing the newly formed plan. This stage requires taking action in the real-world environment.

Taken in sequence, these four stages represent the process of learning. First, direct, concrete engagement with the world generates new experiences, which in turn serve as the basis for reflection. Second, during reflection, additional information is gathered. Third, this new experience, together with the new information, serves to create a new concept or picture of the world. Fourth, the new concept is tested, which creates a new experience, and the cycle is repeated again.

Kolb originally designed the model to describe the individual process of learning. One of the first studies to use Kolb's model to describe the relationship between individual and team learning took place in project development teams at a large consumer products company. Researchers noticed how the processes the teams used to solve problems and develop new products tracked the cycle of learning. First, the teams generated a set of potential solutions to a problem; this is the idea-generating phase of learning. Second, the teams evaluated potential solutions and collected more information on each solution. This suggests a gathering phase of learning. Third, the teams organized all of the available information into a coherent picture. This suggests an organizing phase of team learning. Finally, the team tested the solution to determine if it actually helped in solving the problem, constituting a testing phase (Carlsson, Keane, and Martin, 1976).

Researchers and consultants alike find Kolb's model to be a valuable way to demonstrate the process of learning. Kolb's model relies on retrospective analysis of experience as the source of learning. Indeed, most models of learning require an individual to reflect on his or her experience. But what if individuals or groups had very little time to look back and reflect? How could a team embrace an opportunity for learning in the moment? Unlike the project development teams, the teams on Everest— indeed, many teams involved in life-or-death situations—do not have the luxury to deliberately go through the learning cycle step by step.

Proximal team learning: The TArT approach

To help teams harness opportunities for learning in the moment, a simple but powerful formula has been developed. The model was initially applied to understand how a group of passengers responded when United flight 93 was hijacked by terrorists on September 11, 2001, and eventually crashed into a Pennsylvania cornfield. The passengers' actions seemed to follow the path of the learning cycle: an experience was generated, more information was gathered, a plan of attack was formulated, and action was taken. The learning cycle came into play in a life-or-death situation in an action-directed team (Kayes, 2003).

This model to help groups harness opportunities for learning has been called proximal team learning. *Proximal* means close to or situated near something else. Proximal describes how individuals draw on the knowledge they have within the team, knowledge that is "proximal" to the team. But proximal carries a double meaning: it also refers to the fact that the problem at hand is proximal. The learning is done proximal to the action in time. That is to say that the knowledge draws upon the action it informs. The proximal learning process needs to be done without thought and on the fly, but it cannot simply be intuitive. The process requires systematic thinking in highly dynamic situations. To aid memory in such times and to make the process easy to explain, each stage of the learning cycle has a quick and easy phrase, which can be summarized with the acronym TArT:

▶ Talk it through
▶ Ask around
▶ wRite it down
▶ Try it out.

Talking it through. The emphasis here lies on the spoken word. This means that conversation, not thinking, is the main activity of group learning and development. Thinking is contained within a person's head and it often stays there unless expressed to others in and through language. Talking it through focuses on conversation as learning, as it lets others know what individual members of the group experience. Talking it through helps put words to thoughts, and this leads to new strategies for problem solving. Talking it through represents a process of knowledge generation and corresponds with the concrete experience dimension of the learning process.

During most of the 1996 Everest expeditions, talking it through was nearly impossible. While some guides carried two-way radios, most climbers did not, and the radios used may have been inadequate (Boukreev and DeWalt, 1997). For example, only Fischer and Jangbu carried radios in their team. Thus, once the groups began the final climb to the summit, they had no way to share information, thoughts, observations, or cues. Moreover, the group members did not tie themselves together with ropes in case of a fall, as is customary on difficult climbs. Instead, the groups used fixed ropes, which are attached directly to fixtures on the mountain. These fixed ropes eliminate the need for climbers to depend on one another for support and allow a greater distance to form between members. The lack of radios and the elimination of collective roping meant that the Everest groups could not talk anything through because they were not proximal to each other, nor could they use electronic devices to mediate between experiences.

Asking around. Asking around suggests that valuable information may lie beyond the ranks of the immediate group or any one member. Moving beyond the group to ask around requires the group to go beyond its own mindset and find alternatives that may lead to an increased ability to solve problems. By asking around, the group expands its own boundary (Ancona and Caldwell, 1992). Groups that ask around implicitly understand the limits of their own problem-solving capacity and enlist others to solve a problem. Asking around represents the process of knowledge gathering and corresponds to the reflective observation dimension of learning.

The 1996 Everest climbing season saw nearly 30 groups attempting the summit. Some of these groups met during the first 6 weeks of preparation to coordinate activity, share reports, fix ropes, and establish climbing schedules. Yet as the groups pushed closer to the summit, they appeared to coordinate less and less. New Zealand leader Hall and American leader Fischer both agreed to climb to the summit on the same day, suggesting that these groups asked around to coordinate activity. Yet the agreement they reached—namely, to send Sherpas ahead of the groups to fix ropes—did not occur as planned because Fischer looked the other way as his assistant guide Lopsang Jangbu decided to short-rope, or drag, a weak client to the summit instead. Further, the Taiwanese group ignored the pact made at base camp altogether and attempted to reach the summit on May 9, a day before scheduled. If these groups had asked around, they might have taken more seriously the fact that another group, led by American David Breashears, aborted its May 9th summit attempt to avoid the extensive traffic and the incoming storm suggested by weather reports.

Writing it down. Writing it down implies creating clarity around a set of shared assumptions. Despite the textual nature of the phrase "writing it down," the plan does not have to be literally written on paper. Writing it down implies a set of phrases that can be shared by all members of the group. If these phrases become so ingrained as to guide action, then they become effectively written in the minds of the individuals in the group because they create a common picture or map of the group's plan. Writing it down emphasizes the concrete language used by group members to coordinate action, not a set of abstractions shared among members. In contrast to mental models, writing it down implies a process, not a structure. When groups write it down, they share a process of linking words in a way that creates paradox and alternative. Writing it down represents the knowledge organizing process and corresponds to the abstract conceptualization mode of learning.

Writing it down also serves another purpose: to preserve action in a story that can be used to guide future actions. It is not clear what the

1996 Everest groups had written in their minds, but it does seem apparent that, because they faced a situation that was somewhat unique to the mountain-climbing community (Elmes and Barry, 1999), they may not have developed a language that adequately addressed the complexity of the solution necessary to respond to the problem they faced.

General examples of writing it down can be found in the mountain-climbing community. Several phrases may not be written down expressly but are understood explicitly. Mountain climbers have developed the phrase, "Leave the back door open," to remind themselves that they must balance the demands of getting to the top with the demands of getting back down. When climbers leave the back door open, they pay attention to the route of descent by making both physical and mental markers of the terrain. Leaving the back door open works in concert with another phrase, "Getting to the top is optional, getting down is not," to remind climbing groups that goals can be defined in multiple ways. These phrases are "written" in the minds of climbers and are supported by the climbing community as unwritten rules that guide goal pursuit.

Trying it out. Trying it out suggests that groups must take multiple possible actions to find out what works in various situations. Trying it out suggests that it is not enough to talk about it, ask about it, and write about it; learning also requires action. Trying it out represents the process of putting information into action and corresponds to the active experimentation dimension of learning.

Trying it out seems to be exactly what the groups did during the search for Camp IV and the final rescue of Beck Weathers and Makalu Gau. These groups tried several actions—many of which had never been done before, such as landing a helicopter at 20,000 feet—to find multiple possible solutions to a problem that had never been faced before. Trying it out is a process whereby individuals reconfigure old language in new ways and translate existing processes into new ones. Using Kool-Aid to mark a helicopter landing strip did not require new materials, just the new application of old material. Using a helicopter to lift ailing climbers at high altitude was a new use of old technology. What is new is not the words, or even the process, but rather the configuration of these processes to one another.

The TArT approach to learning helps teams realize the power of learning from experience in the moment. While the TArT model does require retrospective thinking, it provides a quick and easy way to prompt teams to generate opportunities for learning, gather additional information when necessary, formulate a simple but decisive plan, and take immediate action.

Team learning behaviors

To understand the type of learning useful in situations like Everest, a distinction must be made between the various types of team learning. Team learning involves not just one type of behavior, but several inter-related yet distinct behaviors. The distinction between different types of learning is important because not all aspects of learning lead to effectiveness in all situations. When teams successfully navigate the learning cycle, three behaviors will emerge: tacit coordination, adaptation, and collective problem solving.

TACIT COORDINATION

Tacit coordination involves the seamless, often tacit or unconscious, organizing of diverse roles, knowledge, and responsibility in a team. This approach suggests that individuals with varying expertise can coordinate their actions with little communication. Teams that engage in tacit coordination display an almost effortless ability to organize activity and to understand and anticipate the work of other team members. They also interact with other members in a team as needed while displaying the ability to work independently to achieve a team goal.

Tacit coordination is unique from other forms of team learning in that it focuses on the synchronization of knowledge and skills within the team (Klein, 1999). It describes how members can work separately on distinct tasks while being able to synchronize these individual activities with others. Tacit coordination facilitates various teamwork processes such as decision-making, exchange of information, and interpersonal awareness. Tacit coordination is particularly important during short-term projects because teams often do not have the time for the extensive interpersonal or psychological development issues that are typically afforded to teams working together for longer periods of time. Several factors indicate tacit coordination:

▶ understanding the work roles and jobs of other members
▶ accurately anticipating the actions of other members
▶ knowing when to divide individual functions and pool results
▶ working together without thinking about it
▶ showing awareness of the status of a project without checking with other members.

Coordination in action teams often takes years to develop either through training in a team or through individual training in teamwork.

Some action teams, such as firefighters, military teams, and special police units, train in the same team that will eventually carry out the task. This method allows teams to improve synchronization and adjustment. Other teams, however, such as commercial airline cockpit crews, often change team members with each flight. Since the individuals do not train together, the team might lack the important coordination abilities found in teams that train and perform together. Cockpit crews overcome this potential problem by receiving extensive individual training in procedures. These procedures include preflight checklists and standardized rules of interaction so that flight becomes routine.

The Everest teams lacked all of these elements. They did not have extensive individual training, they did not train together for the summit, and they did not have a standardized set of rules or procedures.

ADAPTATION

Adaptive learning describes how teams respond to internal and external demands by adjusting actions and beliefs. Teams that display adaptive learning act decisively in the face of challenges or threats and respond to new situations as they arise. Whereas tacit cooperation focuses on how individuals work together and thus improve team and individual learning, adaptation focuses on how teams respond to changes and constraints. Adaptation is demonstrated when a team can evaluate its processes, change directions, and develop a new course of action in response to perceived threats or inadequacies with the current problem-solving strategy.

Adaptive learning has a rich tradition within the study of organizations and management. This adapting perspective suggests that teams need to adjust to environmental changes, such as the implementation of new technology (Edmondson, Bohmer, and Pisano, 2001). Teams that are adapting may proactively identify mistakes and correct them before they occur. Adapting is an important part of learning in short-term project teams. The ability to adapt to changing demands in the external environment may allow teams to make sense of the world around them. Short-term teams often face single, relatively stable, but not necessarily well-structured tasks. Several factors indicate adaptation:

▶ knowing how to react when faced with a new problem
▶ knowing what to do if something goes wrong with a project
▶ responding to new issues as they arise
▶ moving into action when faced with an unexpected problem
▶ not repeating the same mistake.

COLLECTIVE PROBLEM SOLVING

Collective problem solving, as a form of learning, describes how teams direct their attention to related activities that address specific and defined problems. Collective problem solving focuses on the nature of the problem and the group's method for solving the problem. One approach to collective problem solving focuses on the team's cognitive complexity or the degree to which teams learn to think in a more complex way (Gruenfeld and Hollingshead, 1993). Collective problem solving also includes adapting to new demands, but it remains more concerned with the attention on and activity of problem solving itself.

Experiential approaches to team learning suggest that teams exercise considerable discretion over how they interpret their tasks (Kayes, Kayes, and Kolb, 2005). Collective problem solving involves sharing knowledge about the current situation that may aid in accomplishing the task. Collective problem solving is likely to improve performance when the knowledge required to complete a task requires continual updating based on changes in the environment or condition of the team. Problem solving as learning is especially important when a task embodies more complexity than the expertise of any one individual who can master working alone. Several factors indicate collective problem solving:

▶ finding several alternatives to solve a problem
▶ talking about how to solve problems
▶ talking about how to improve
▶ finding and correcting mistakes before they happen
▶ evaluating processes and mistakes.

Team learning and goals

As explained in Chapter 7, teamwork involves developing a set of shared beliefs among team members—related to goal sharing, interpersonal understanding, trust, and possibly team efficacy. These core teamwork processes lead to or facilitate the team learning behaviors described above: tacit coordination, adaptation, and problem solving.

When teams adopt these shared beliefs and engage in these behaviors, they begin to develop a more complex goal structure that allows them to respond to changing situations within the team and in its environment. Kayes, Kayes, and Kolb (2005) suggest that the process of developing a complex goal structure is not happenstance. It occurs when the teams have a learning orientation, and it can be facilitated by leadership.

A complex goal structure means, in most cases, that the goals that are established and pursued include emotional and practical considerations. A goal is not as simple as "reaching the top of the mountain," but incorporates often conflicting goals such as "reaching the top of the mountain and getting back down." The distinction between these two goals seems both trite and obvious, but the distinction often gets lost when goal-setting is not accompanied by an ethic of learning.

One reason setting and pursuing complex goals may be so difficult is that leaders often fail to consider the competing demands and commitments inherent in human activity. Goals are not always rational, and the goal-setting process is filled with challenges often overlooked when the initial goal was set. What Everest climber would have considered the eclectic mix of climbers that appeared on Everest in 1996, when they first set out to summit Everest? What leader would have foreseen getting lost in the summit and failing to enforce turnaround times? Goals and the challenges necessary to achieve them evolve over time, and leaders who embrace learning can more effectively respond to these demands and alter their course of action.

Kayes, Kayes, and Kolb (2005) described challenges involved during goal development. For example, early on, a team will confront differences between individual and team goals. It will have to gain clarity about the team goal and achieve alignment between individual and team goals. Later, as a team achieves higher levels of functioning, it will develop an overall goal shared by all members, continually redefine and change goals as circumstances change, and attract new members to the goal to perpetuate the team's purpose.

A team that learns will be able to respond to the changing internal and external demands of its environment and ultimately be on its way to overcome destructive goal pursuit. A team that learns will be able to maximize the benefits of goals by developing a complex goal structure.

The goal development process

As demonstrated by the teams led by Hall and Fischer, leading a team in achieving goals is seldom systematic. Further, teams often fail to fully realize the potential of the goal-setting process. Yet, an initial understanding of the process of goal development can be achieved through a systematic model of goal development in teams. The following model suggests that team goals can be structured in terms of five continuous phases, each with its own challenges. As a team works through each phase, it becomes more proficient in achieving higher team functioning (Kayes, Kayes, and Kolb, 2005).

PHASE 1: INDIVIDUAL PURPOSE

In Phase 1, team members come together for individual purposes. The group simply serves as the means to accomplish the goal. For example, because mounting an expedition to summit Everest requires a great deal of resources, individuals join an expedition where resources can be pooled together, costs can reach an economy of scale, and individuals can support each other.

PHASE 2: SUSTAINED PURPOSE

In Phase 2, team members work together to sustain their pursuit of the goal. It is important to remember here that goals are not yet shared; individuals continue to pursue their own goals, with the team simply providing a sustained means or context in which to pursue the goals. For example, members of Hall's and Fischer's expedition teams continued to stay with the expedition because they believed being a part of the expedition would help them realize their individual goals. In contrast, members of the South African expedition, led by Ian Woodall, abandoned their pursuit altogether or continued their pursuit independent of the other team members.

PHASE 3: INDIVIDUAL PURPOSE TO SERVE THE TEAM

In Phase 3 of team goal development, individual goals become modified in order to serve the collective goal of the team. Individuals will begin to contribute resources to the group rather than just focus resources on achieving their own goal in the context of the group.

PHASE 4: TEAM-DRIVEN PURPOSE

In Phase 4, the team itself will begin to modify its goals in order to fit the team's desired direction. Phase 4 marks the first time the group begins to set the goal rather than being driven by individual goals. In this phase, individuals not only pursue the group goal but become willing to abandon their own individual goals in order to achieve the greater goal of the group.

PHASE 5: MULTIPLE-GOAL TEAM

In Phase 5, the highest development of group goals occurs, allowing groups to pursue multiple goals simultaneously. Teams that foster multiple goals have a number of characteristics. One characteristic is the ability to change goals in response to a rapidly changing environment. Teams functioning at this high level constantly assess and redefine their goal based on new information and changes in the environment. New goals emerge. Old goals are replaced and accepted by all team members, and actions reflect these changes. A second characteristics of these teams is that they then hold multiple—often competing—goals.

Goal-setting on Everest

One reason the teams led by Hall and Fischer walked into trouble was because they continued to operate as individuals—with individual goals. The team members continued to work as individuals, at Phase 2, despite the need for a more complex set of team goals. Indeed, some members functioned within a more complex goal structure. For example, the assistant team leaders did devote resources to getting other members down safely, but as a whole, few team members were willing to devote resources to the success of the team, as can be seen in Krakauer's reluctance to help fix ropes during the final push to the summit. Not until after the leaders became severed from the teams did the teams begin to display goals with a more complex structure, such as Phases 3 through 5 mentioned above.

Consideration of the phases of goal pursuit helps highlight yet another aspect of goalodicy. Goalodicy may arise when teams pursue complex goals but have not developed an appropriate goal structure. When teams operate in Phases 1 through 3, but the goal environment requires operating in levels 4 and 5, goalodicy is likely to set in.

In summary, in the early stages of team development, team members simply focus on using the team as a means to achieving their goal. As teams develop, they begin to develop shared goals where members devote individual resources to achieve collective or team-level goals. To help teams learn and develop, leaders can foster a team environment where learning thrives. Leaders can also promote learning by having teams engage in learning behaviors, encourage proximal processes, and provide opportunities for teams to fail and recover. The box below provides a comprehensive view of the team learning processes that lead to higher team functioning.

A COMPREHENSIVE APPROACH TO TEAM LEARNING

Higher team functioning

A situation in which individual team members realize the positive bene-fits of goals and the goal-setting process by developing a complex goal structure.

Indicators of higher functioning teams

- ▶ **Members understand and accept differences in individual goals**
- ▶ **Members spend time talking about emotional and goal-related issues but preserve conflict for goal-related issues**
- ▶ **Members foster multiple goals**
- ▶ **Members constantly assess and redefine their goal based on new information and changes in the environment**
- ▶ **Members often hold competing or complementary goals, but this does not inhibit progress**
- ▶ **Members have a greater awareness of others' expectations and goals**

Team shared beliefs that lead to higher functioning

- ▶ **Interpersonal understanding**
- ▶ **Trust**
- ▶ **Goal sharing**
- ▶ **Efficacy**

Team learning behaviors that lead to higher functioning

- ▶ **Tacit coordination**
- ▶ **Adaptation**
- ▶ **Problem solving**

Team knowledge gathering and processing that lead to higher functioning

- ▶ **Talking it through (concrete experience)**
- ▶ **Asking around (reflective observation)**
- ▶ **Writing it down (abstract conceptualization)**
- ▶ **Trying it out (active experimentation)**

While Everest provides a unique context for understanding teamwork, it also provides insight into a few common misunderstandings about leadership. The next chapter explores the notion that learning requires some leadership skills that have been largely ignored by current thinking on leadership.

Learning points

▶ Opportunities for learning present themselves at every turn. An examination of how the Everest teams learned from these opportunities illustrates how team learning provides the key to navigating complex and changing circumstances.
▶ Learning involves a four-step process of experience, reflection, abstraction, and action. Proximal team learning uses this model to describe an easy four-step process for learning in teams: Talking it through, Asking around, wRiting it down, and Trying it out, or the TArT approach to learning in action. Each phase of the model corresponds to the four-step process of learning.
▶ Team learning requires a team to be well formed and to have adopted the shared beliefs that facilitate teamwork as discussed in the previous chapter. Three behaviors associated with team learning are tacit coordination, adaptation, and collective problem solving.
▶ Team goals have five phases: (1) individual purpose; (2) sustained purpose; (3) individual purpose to serve the team; (4) team-driven purpose; and (5) multiple-goal team.
▶ Once team members begin to learn, they can then begin to work as a higher-functioning team.

Learning questions

▶ The chapter outlines a number of times the Everest teams took advantage of opportunities for learning. Can you think of additional times the teams took advantage of learning? Why do you think this chapter focused on the learning opportunities that occurred during the descent from the summit?
▶ Think of a time when you learned as a team. What was the team like? What conditions in the team promoted team learning?
▶ Think of a team you have either observed or taken part in. Did the team demonstrate any of the three team learning processes mentioned here—tacit coordination, adaptation, or collective problem solving?

9 Beyond Goals: Overcoming Destructive Goal Pursuit Through Learning

Once you have obtained your goal, you reflect back on what occurred and realized that you overlooked important, life-threatening details. You reached the summit and achieved your goal, but you did so at a cost. The cost included the lives of other team members, the time you committed to reaching the summit that you could have spent on other productive pursuits, and the suffering of those who love you as they waited to hear about your fate.

You think about the decisions you made in the face of pursuing the summit and how the goal guided your behavior, how the goal drove you to continue, how the goal limited what information you gathered during the pursuit, and how you processed that information. You think about how the goal provided justification for action.

Reflecting back on your experience, you learned some things about yourself and the goal-setting process. Perhaps you made a decision to turn back just short of the summit and now you consider how you will evaluate your pursuit. Perhaps you continued to the summit, taking considerable risk to your life, and now you consider the logic of that decision. Perhaps your decisions had an impact on your teammates, and you reflect upon the group dynamics that transpired. Either way, you now must re-evaluate your goals and consider how to put yourself back together. You are one of the survivors, but you must still pay the price of being part of a team that broke down while pursuing a goal. Some consideration of what went wrong and how to prevent this kind of fiasco from occurring again becomes essential to living with yourself. An evaluation of the situation will help you be more realistic, safer, and successful in the future pursuit of goals.

The previous two chapters expressed the importance of teamwork and team learning for managing the goal-setting process in complex situations. These chapters argued the importance of establishing certain shared beliefs among team members that facilitate the productive pursuit of goals. This chapter builds on the ideas of teamwork and team learning

Table 4 **Seven processes that lead to productive goal pursuit**

Process	Description
Recognizing ill-structured problems	Define the problem faced broadly enough to consider multiple outcomes and unintended consequences of action
Learning from experience	Develop multiple strategies for achieving goals, assess impact, and update with new strategies, especially under novel situations
Engaging in recovery	Develop mechanisms to adjust to setbacks, mistakes, and errors
Fostering trust	Develop a culture safe for surfacing problems
Developing tacit coordination	Foster tacit coordination among team members, which promotes learning
Minding the gap	Attend to discrepancies among present reality and ideal expectations
Cultivating multiple goals	Develop multiple often competing goals that reflect the complexity of the situation faced

to present specific actions for team leaders to take to foster team learning during the goal-setting process (Table 4). This chapter draws on a variety of sources and uses examples of teams engaged in a variety of settings, including combat, commercial flights, and business.

These processes provide leaders with specific beliefs and behaviors that can lead to improved goal-setting in the face of complex situations. Observation of many teams in a variety of high-pressure situations, including the mountain climbers on Everest in 1996, reveals that developing a more complex goal structure within the team results in a more flexible, yet more resilient, goal-directed team. These seven processes foster positive goal pursuit and forestall the onset of goalodicy.

Recognizing ill-structured problems

To effectively achieve a goal, the goal must first be defined adequately. In most cases, "summit a mountain" is a fairly well-defined problem. After all, one of the most compelling reasons for pursuing the summit rests in the idea that the goal is clear: reaching the top. Yet, in 1996 a number of factors increased the complexity of the situation so that successfully defining the goal was more complex. To achieve a better set of goals, a better understanding of the nature of goal-setting is essential. Most importantly, it is important to clarify the nature of the problem faced. This requires distinguishing between a well-defined and an ill-defined problem. An ill-defined problem carries at least three characteristics (King and Kitchener, 1994).

THE GOAL IS UNCLEAR

The first characteristic of an ill-defined problem is that the nature of the goal itself is unclear. Exactly what is to be obtained or sought is not evident from the start. The suggestion that getting to the top of the mountain describes an unclear goal seems strange. Yet, too many expedition teams, including the teams led by Fischer, Hall, and Gau in 1996, rested on the assumption that the goal was clear. A deeper look at the goal, however, suggests that it was not clear if the teams believed that reaching the summit was most important—rather than reaching the summit and getting back down. As an experienced Himalayan guide, Jim Williams knows the ill-defined nature of Everest expeditions. He writes,

> You're not paid to summit Everest. You're paid to get people to the summit of Everest safely and return them safely. A case in point was last year.... We turned around and went down with everybody [b]ecause we could not come up with a timeline that was gonna allow us to safely summit and return with these people with sufficient oxygen before it got dark.... There's some disappointed people but they're alive and disappointed. That's what the $65,000 [fee to join an expedition] is for. (Outside Online, 1997)

David Breashears, an experienced climber and high-altitude film-maker, knows the importance of leading complex expeditions. Breashears contends that leaders often get confused about the nature of their goal during the pursuit. When you lead a team on the world's highest peaks, Breashears says,

> And you're not thinking clearly and not making the best decisions and I think you just get a little bit confused, but—and you may have lost sight of the fact that your obligation is not, as a guide, to get somebody up a mountain, it's to make sure they return safely with all their fingers and toes. You know, your only real obligation is to the welfare of your clients. (Rose, 1997)

Each of these statements by experienced and successful expedition team leaders implies that learning communicates a sense of the complexity of the situation. Success is not just defined in terms of getting to the top.

Success includes the safety of climbers and a broader understanding that getting to the summit is one of many goals that need to be achieved.

THE MEANS TO ACHIEVE THE GOAL ARE UNCLEAR

If the goal itself lacks clarity during ill-defined problem solving, then so does the means to achieve the goal. On Everest, no one really agreed on the best strategy to reach the summit. Despite years of climbing Everest and over 1000 successful summits, reaching the summit and getting back down safely may rely on a few simple judgments. In the final analysis, solving ill-structured problems cannot be boiled down to a few simple rules but exists in the judgments brought about by experience and the attitude of learning.

Ed Viesturs knows the ill-structured nature of defining and pursuing challenging goals. As the first American to reach the summit of the world's 14 highest mountains, Viesturs makes these kinds of judgments on a regular basis. Viesturs comments on the muddiness of the decision-making process. He states:

> There's so many things that went wrong—little errors, things that are black and white down here aren't really black and white up there. You know, the decision-making process is a little bit more muddled. (Rose, 1998)

EXPERTS DISAGREE

The third characteristic of an ill-structured problem rests in the nature of success. If a problem is ill-structured, whether or not success is achieved will be disputed among experts. It seems strange to suggest that success in mountain climbing lacks clarity: you either reach the summit or you do not. Again, the temptation is to oversimplify. Take, for example, the dispute that has existed over whether Mallory actually reached the summit in 1924 and whether it really matters if Mallory did not get back down safely. In the case of Mallory, it is not clear if he and his climbing partner reached the summit. One element of the debate rests on whether he died on his descent. Another element of the debate rests on whether or not it would count as "successful" since the team did not make it back down.

The issue with each of these problems is that traditional approaches to goal-setting fail to account for the unintended consequences of reaching goals. By defining goals narrowly and absolutely, leaders and teams fail to account for the unintended consequences, even when those consequences are severe. Does getting to the summit of the mountain satisfy the need to achieve a goal if the climber dies while getting down?

Thus, the first step to an effective goal-setting process is to recognize the ill-structured nature of the problem. Leaders will be better able to engage in goal-setting when they recognize that goal-setting in the face of an ill-defined problem involves unclear outcomes, unclear processes, and lack of consensus over success. This basic understanding of the nature of the problem will help leaders decide whether they should engage followers in learning or performance modes to reach the goal.

Learning from experience

Setting goals in the face of ill-defined problems requires learning, especially when the task is new and the means to achieve the goal are unclear. The first ascent of Everest, which occurred in 1953 when Edmond Hillary and Tenzing Norgay reached the summit, is instructive. Hillary and Norgay worked as a team, climbing together for the lead up to the final push for the summit. In fact, analysis of the distances they covered leading up to the final push to the summit shows that Norgay and Hillary actually covered the distance to the summit three-and-a-half times (Miller, 2003). This experience served a broader purpose than just conditioning and adjustment to the high altitude. The repetition served as the basis for experience. Norgay and Hillary's attempt was consistent with other attempts at the summit in that they used a small group, usually two climbers, carrying only essential supplies with them to the summit. This approach is called the "Alpine style" because it was developed by climbers in the Alps. By following the same method that other, unsuccessful teams followed, the teams of climbers were trying to draw on the lessons of prior climbers. In other words, they were learning from the experiences of those who had failed.

In the first successful ascent of Everest, learning must have dominated the landscape. The expedition teams were deciphering new situations, identifying and trying new routes, and deciding when to abandon them. The expedition drew on lessons learned from previous ill-fated expeditions like those of Mallory and Irvine, which left them both dead. It is well understood that the successful 1953 British Expedition learned from the 1952 Swiss expedition. The Swiss were given exclusive rights to Everest and had reached higher than any previous expedition on Everest. But with the weather turning colder and a storm blowing in, the team abandoned their summit after reaching 28,300 feet. In 1953, the British captured the knowledge of the Swiss expedition by hiring Tenzing Norgay, known as "the most remarkable of all the Sherpas" (Clark, 1976, p. 187). The successful British expedition also captured the oxygen bottles, food, and some equipment left behind by the Swiss.

First ascents require learning and the development of new strategies because the task of reaching the summit is novel. These strategies might include clocking estimated ascent and descent times to establish turn-around times and monitoring and logging weather patterns and route details. Ultimately, solving ill-defined problems requires that leaders take advantage of the various opportunities for learning from experience.

An example of learning from experience occurred when an experienced mountain climber, such as Ed Viesturs, becomes alarmed when other climbers ignore pre-established turnaround times. Sensing that something is wrong, he seeks more information. The same thing occurs outside of mountain climbing: a doctor may notice that a patient has an unusual pain, unrelated to her current diagnosis. He recognizes a pattern between this patient and other patients. He does not quite know what is causing the pain, but he foregoes a less-invasive surgery in favor of a more invasive one. He conducts the more invasive surgery because he senses a greater problem, even though he cannot quite explain it through the existing tests. The more invasive surgery reveals what the less invasive approach would not. The woman has experienced an accumulation of problems, brought about by the initial problem.

In these examples, leaders take initial information from the environment and then use their initial hunch to obtain more information. The hunch is based on experience. For example, the surgeon's work with past patients reveals a pattern that is shared by this woman, and the climber's knowledge of turnaround times tells him that something is wrong with continued pursuit. But notice that experience is not enough. There is a difference between learning from experience and simply relying on exper-ience. When leaders learn from experience, it means that experience serves as the basis for future exploration. By contrast, when leaders rely on exper-ience, they stop seeking new information after their hunch. The initial hunch is simply confirmed, not used as the basis for additional discovery.

Learning from experience becomes possible when leaders develop a system that allows for recovery every time a hunch occurs.

Engaging in recovery

Leaders that encourage learning from experience create mechanisms to deal with setbacks and problems encountered during goal pursuit. The key issue here is that teams put mechanisms in place to respond to setbacks when they occur. And setbacks will occur when a team faces ill-defined problems. A better understanding of what it means to engage in recovery stems from debates on human error.

ON HUMAN ERROR

Up to this point, the term *error* has not been used to describe the events and behaviors of leaders on Everest. Errors are typically defined as deviations from expected outcomes. It has become commonplace to use the language of errors to describe how people's behavior deviates from expectations. It may be appropriate to talk about errors in many circumstances, such as in hospitals and nuclear power plants, but in many cases of leadership the term does not fully explain what occurred. In Everest, as well as some other situations, the language of errors lulls us into thinking about leadership in an unproductive way.

To explain why such terminology is unproductive, a brief turn is required to an interesting but relatively little known line of thinking that comes from the research of breakdowns in complex situations. Jens Rasmussen (1990) has spent years thinking about the breakdown of complex systems like nuclear power plants. While Rasmussen's thinking has mostly informed research on how people deal with highly complex and technical systems, his work is informative for the present conversation on leadership. Rasmussen helps us see one of the limits of our current thinking about the role of leadership in the face of ill-defined problems.

Calling a discrepancy an error is appropriate when the problem is well defined, when the situation is stable and predictable. Goals help focus efforts toward a specific, measurable, and achievable outcome, and focused effort tends to improve performance in such stable situations. But this focused effort means that work processes become fixed. Fixed and stable actions mean that learning and exploration of an alternative course of action decrease. Too much focus on a single, narrow goal will inevitably stifle learning. As a situation changes and conditions become more dynamic, the original goal becomes inadequate. The narrow goal can no longer match the complexity of the new situation. When a situation shifts and becomes more dynamic, a leader can no longer rely on the usual cues to be valid (see Weick, Sutcliffe, and Obstfeld, 1999). This is the situation that produces "errors." Errors emerge when current routines meet unexpected situations.

The conventional wisdom would ask: How can leaders help themselves and their team members avoid errors? If we take this question to heart, we would think that leaders need to learn how to avoid errors. But conventional wisdom supplies the wrong question. Rasmussen believes that errors have a purpose. Errors create opportunities for learning. Without errors, systems cannot learn. Eliminate errors and learning grinds to a halt. As one scholar noted back in 1905, "Knowledge and error flows from the same mental sources, only success can tell the one from the other" (cited in Rasmussen, 1988, p. 25).

Here lies Rasmussen's most important point: rather than trying to eliminate error, systems should focus on developing mechanisms to recover from errors. Errors are an inevitable part of complex systems anyway. In short, Rasmussen suggests that systems need not eliminate errors—eliminating errors would be impossible—but they should seek mechanisms to respond to and learn from errors as they occur.

Thinking in terms of recovery from error, rather than avoidance of error, lends important insight into leadership. The primary role of the leader is not to direct actions of others toward goals, but rather to direct others toward learning. Learning to recover from the unexpected becomes the primary goal of leadership. To facilitate recovery from errors, leaders need to be aware of the individual's capacity for knowledge processing and the degree of discretion the team member has for operating within the system.

LEARNING FROM ERRORS: FACTORS RELATED TO INDIVIDUALS

The first set of factors for helping teams think in terms of recovery focuses on the individual—specifically, the particular knowledge processing capacity of individual team members. Knowledge processing involves knowledge, competence, and access.

Knowledge of the situation

First, individual team members must have knowledge that allows them to respond effectively as new situations arise. When team members share knowledge of the situation, they each possess important pieces of information. In analyzing Everest, for example, we might ask the following question: *Did team members know about the turnaround times?* Several pieces of evidence suggest that all team members knew about turnaround times, at least in general. Videotape taken at base camp shows that leaders Hall and Fischer talked about turnaround times, and several of the climbers mentioned turnaround times in their accounts of events. The first consideration for leading recovery is that team members have the necessary knowledge to assess a situation. Having knowledge of a situation is closely tied to competence in how to handle it: although knowledge and competence are not the same thing, having knowledge is the first step to being able to respond.

Competence

The individual must have the competence to respond to situations as they arise. In other words, the individual must have the capacity to make an "educated" decision about how to respond. Whether this ability to make an educated decision comes from formal training, experience, or a combination of both, having the cognitive capacity to assess the situation and make a decision lies as much in interpreting the situation as it does in any objective view of the world. The competence question on Everest would be, *Did the team members have the ability to abandon their summit attempts when a turnaround time came and went?*

Competence to act was demonstrated by a group of climbers, including Lou Kasischke, who chose to abandon their summit attempt at about 11:00 because they determined that their progress to that point would not allow them to safely get to the summit and return. Kasischke believed he had the necessary authority and ability to abandon his approach. He recounts the decision to return to camp and forgo the summit.

> We felt, because of the bottleneck delay and our 1 p.m. turnaround time, that it was too late to go to the summit, and would therefore be too risky coming back down. I didn't rescue anyone, and on summit day did nothing I can take pride in – except that at the critical moment I exercised the personal responsibility that each of us had and made a decision to turn around. (in Coburn, 1997, p. 192)

Kasischke's comment suggest that members of Hall's team had both knowledge of the situation and the ability to act independently of the rest of the team. Kasischke's decision was different from the decision of Doug Hansen. According to Kasischke, Hansen expressed his desire to abandon his attempt and join those descending. Hansen said he felt tired. Yet, in the end, Hansen must have changed his mind because he continued up with Hall to the summit (Coburn, 1997, p. 196).

However, neither general knowledge nor competence alone is enough; team members must have access to timely information.

Access to timely information

Access to timely information is often a problem in teams because leaders often have access to information that is unavailable to the team members. As each group of climbers pushed for the summit, they likely did so knowing very little about the progress of other climbers, the impending storm, or the lack of fixed ropes, which would slow down their progress. This third consideration lies in the notion that what is known and what is not known is based on time. In other words, when team members know something and when they do not is an important consideration as well. The essential question that should be asked by the Everest leaders is *Do team members have access to the information they need to decide whether they should turn around and abandon the summit at this point in time?*

After witnessing the deaths of the eight climbers, IMAX expedition leader David Breashears describes the decision of his team to postpone their final push for the summit for later in the week.

> And so we went down. It wasn't a difficult decision because it wasn't a final one. We weren't going home, just down. It wasn't my call alone. I talked with [fellow team members] Ed [Viesturs] and Robert [Schauer] that morning, and we all came to the same quite, sober conclusion. Ed felt very strongly that the weather was still unsettled—that our window hadn't arrived. There was nothing to be lost by going down except a little bit of pride and some time, which wasn't yet crucial. . . . Once the decision was made, we simply disengaged from our goal. (Breashears, 1999, p. 252)

The need for team member knowledge, competence, and access to timely information suggests that the wisdom of recovery lies in the hand of individual team members, not in the leaders. No leader, no matter how knowledgeable, competent, or informed, can solely manage the recovery process. Leaders must develop the ability of team members to respond individually or as a team. Team leaders can facilitate recovery in their team members by developing individual team members. In the end, no amount of training or development will be enough unless team leaders can help teams deal with a second set of factors related to recovery.

LEARNING FROM ERRORS: FACTORS RELATED TO THE TASK

To learn from errors, another set of factors is required to address how an individual team member relates to his or her job or task. First, in situations of ill-structured problem solving, individuals must have discretion over the process needed to solve the problem. When ill-structured problems exist, actions need to be left open to the discretion of trained and experienced team members. Team members, and not just leaders, need to be able to exercise judgment.

Individuals also need to know various strategies that can be taken to confront a problem, and they need to be given the discretion to change course based on their interpretation of events at a particular time.

EXAMPLE OF RECOVERY: RESCUE AT 20,000 FEET

The rescue of dying climbers Beck Weathers and Makalu Gau by Nepalese helicopter pilot Madan K. C. on May 13 provides a good example of elements necessary for recovery during ill-structured problem solving. The U.S. Embassy urged the Nepalese government to send a helicopter to rescue Weathers and Gau. Madan, who had trained with the U.S. Army in Miami, Florida, agreed to the challenge of attempting the world's highest rescue attempt only after two commercial pilots declined. When Madan first brought his helicopter to the high camp, he probably knew that no small helicopter had landed at this altitude since 1973. He also probably knew that one of the helicopters that flew in 1973 crashed into the mountain.

Yet, Madan was not acting without knowledge of the situation he faced. From his prior experience, he knew that weather, weight, and lift would be important variables in the successful rescue. The weather needed to hold long enough to get into the landing spot as well as to get out. In the Himalayas, clouds can form quickly, and almost all flights in and out of the mountains are done through visuals of the pilots. Even with a clear sky, flying in the mountains is a dangerous game. Without a clear sky, flying is nearly impossible. Over the years, many helicopters have been lost to "controlled flight into terrain," or CFIT. This occurs when a pilot loses the ability to correctly judge position and unknowingly flies right into a mountainside.

Madan knew that a clearing in the clouds was not enough to get the climbers to safety; his helicopter needed to be able to lift off the ground with the added weight of the ailing climber. Helicopters are extremely sensitive to weight. With a few pounds of extra weight, a helicopter is not likely to get off the ground. So Madan left Katmandu and then dropped off his copilot and all but 5 gallons of fuel at about 18,000 feet before heading up the mountain.

It is not clear that Madan even knew where to land when he arrived. Since no helicopters had flown that high, no landing pad existed. What was going through his mind when he saw a landing pad marked in Kool-Aid powder must not have been too encouraging. One of the rescue party members, David Breashears, found a small strip on the iceberg. Breashears had worked on a number of films that included helicopters. Madan had to make two passes across the makeshift pad and then finally hovered to the ground. But as he slowly brought his helicopter to the makeshift landing pad, he kept the rooters of his machine in motion as the rescue team quickly put the first climber in the bay of his copter. "There was no place for us to land but somehow, we managed and picked up the climbers," Madan told reporters (CNN, 1996). He signaled to the rescue team that he could only take one climber because two climbers would not allow him to obtain and maintain enough lift in his helicopter to fly down. Within seconds, the helicopter took off, only to return about 45 minutes later to pick up the second climber (see Krakauer, 1997a, p. 264).

In summary, the most important consideration in thinking recovery is that recovery happens at the level of individual team members. It is at this level that recovery will be most successful. By the time most problems reach the leaders, it will be too late. It will be too late to make a successful recovery and, more importantly, too late to be able to discern the proper actions to take. In order to think recovery, team leaders must increase the individual team members' capacity for knowledge and create an environment where team members can respond to small discrepancies that they notice so that a response can occur before the problem reaches the leader. To build an environment where thinking recovery is possible, leaders must create an open and psychologically safe environment, which involves fostering a culture of trust.

Fostering trust

Feeling safe to talk about problems or perceived problems is a critical component of effective goal pursuit. Trust, a shared belief among members, is demonstrated as much by perceptions as by actions. We move beyond the mountain-climbing community to find an example of how trust can be fostered.

Amy Edmonson is a professor at Harvard and one of the foremost authorities on team learning. Edmondson (2003) studied how surgery teams learned to use a newly developed, minimally invasive procedure for heart surgery. Under conventional procedures, doctors crack open the patient's breastbone. With the new minimally invasive procedure, operating teams work through small incisions made between the rib bones of the patient. The patient recovery time for this new procedure is much shorter than for conventional procedures.

One major implication for the surgery is the interdependency required of the team members, since the head surgeons rely on nurses and other assistants to read information from a monitor. A process that previously relied heavily on the surgeon's skill alone now relied on a team of people (Edmondson, 2003, p. 1427). Edmondson highlighted several qualities that improved performance in this environment by promoting trust: fostering inclusiveness, minimizing power differences, and communicating humility.

FOSTERING INCLUSIVENESS

Edmondson and her colleagues found that team leaders (i.e., the surgeons directing the procedures) who fostered trust in their groups by encouraging other team members to actively participate performed better and learned more quickly than leaders who did not foster such an environment. The most effective team leaders fostered trust by taking on a coaching orientation during practice rounds. The leaders set the tone during practice sessions when lives were not at stake by fostering the inclusiveness of all team members.

The best-performing teams had leaders that focused on learning rather than doing things the same way. The surgeons talked about the importance of the procedures, the willingness of participants to learn the new procedures, and the need for training as a key element of the new procedures. Importantly, the effective team leaders communicated the advantages of the new procedures as well as the need to prepare for the training.

In contrast, the less-effective team leaders showed little interest in the procedures beyond their economic or competitive value. Some less-effective team leaders even expressed disinterest in the value of the new procedures. The less-effective leaders failed to motivate those around them about the importance of learning the new procedures.

MINIMIZING POWER DIFFERENCES

Leaders of the top-performing teams also minimized power differences and emphasized teamwork over individual ability in learning about the new technology. The power differences were minimized in two ways. First, the leader asked for the input of others and took action based on those inputs. Second, the leader suggested that the individual contribution of team members was essential for the success of the team (Edmondson, 2003, p. 1439). Edmondson quotes one of the top surgeons: "The whole model of surgeons barking orders down from on high is gone. There is a whole new wave of interaction.... The ability of the surgeon to allow himself [sic] to become a partner not a dictator is critical" (Edmondson, 2003, p. 1440).

COMMUNICATING HUMILITY

The third behavior demonstrated by team leaders involved communicating their own need to learn as individuals.

Surgeons face extreme situations where outcomes can lead to disaster and death. The important message from Edmondson's research is that if surgeons can learn to be more inclusive and less authoritative and can foster trust, then other leaders can as well.

Rob Hall, the New Zealand team leader, might have acted differently had he known the importance of minimizing power differences. In a short sequence of amateur videotape taken at base camp prior to the summit, Hall proclaimed: "Maybe I'll get unpopular, but somebody has to be unpopular sometimes" (ABC News, 1996b, p. 2). The IMAX team leader David Breashears was "taken aback" by Hall's authoritarian stance. Breashears (1999) recounts Hall's claim as the unofficial enforcer of garbage control at base camp. Hall quipped "I don't mind being the mountain's policeman," he said. "I'm a great guy to have as a friend, but I'm a bad person to have as your enemy. If anyone leaves garbage on the mountain, even so much as leaves one paper wrapper, you're going to answer to me" (Breashears, 1999, p. 241).

Hall's use of authority provides an important contrast with the effective surgical teams mentioned above.

Developing tacit coordination

Teams that learn to coordinate the actions of individual team members have acquired important skills that will help them achieve their goals and re-evaluate them when necessary. As discussed in Chapter 7, coordinating action involves an almost seamless ability to communicate, anticipate, and respond to the actions of other team members. Teams that face life-and-death situations and confront complex, ill-structured problems improve on their ability to successfully reach goals when they coordinate action.

Coordinated action appears to be a common feature of teams that perform well in high-stress situations. Lt Colonel Nate Allen teaches leadership at the U.S. Military Academy at West Point. His interest lies in understanding and helping infantry leaders to learn, especially during the difficult and confusing times of combat. Colonel Allen (2006) traveled to the danger zones of Iraq in 2005 to study leaders in a highly complex and risky environment, one of the most trying leadership situations imaginable.

One of the leaders he studied was a helicopter pilot who flew support for an infantry unit stationed in a difficult location in Iraq. The pilot explains the near-effortless coordination with his ground unit.

The relationship we had with the ground unit we were supporting in the area was amazing. We had operated together long enough where my guys knew by the sound of the ground unit leaders' voices who they were, and they knew ours. We were able to operate together with very little coordination, because we understood each other so well. (Allen, 2006)

The pilot's words clearly illustrate several aspects of coordinated action. First, the team membership involved strong "relationships" that were probably built over a period of experiences. The team members "knew by the sound of the ground unit leaders' voices who they were, and they knew us." This suggests a sense of familiarity with other members. This familiarity probably led to the ability to anticipate other members' actions.

The pilot's statement also illustrates confidence that other members will come through with their anticipated action. This aspect of team functioning is important: it allows team members to worry less about whether other members are following through with their plan and to concentrate more on their own individual responsibility. In a team with less coordination, team members need to constantly monitor the work of others for fear that a key task will be left undone.

As the pilot stated, his team was "able to operate together with very little coordination, because [team members] understood each other so well." In a highly coordinated team, the teamwork aspect of the team becomes almost second nature, allowing team members to focus on the situation at hand—and to be aware of and take advantage of opportunities for learning.

The pilot's comments show an irony of team coordinating action: the more a team coordinates action, the less it needs to coordinate action. More coordination eventually leads to less need to coordinate. Thus, the most effective teams—teams that can learn and work effectively in a constantly changing, multiple-goal environment—require less coordination than teams that are less effective.

CROSS-TEAM COORDINATION

Effective coordinated action requires coordinating not just within each team or unit, but among teams and units as well. Colonel Allen discovered the need for cross-team coordination in his research. One commander of an armored division talked about how coordination among all teams in his unit proved just as important as coordination within his own team. Enemy insurgents did not distinguish between teams; they saw all soldiers as the enemy. He stated:

In studying ourselves we've got to talk with each other because I might be varying my routes and observation post locations, but if one of my sister units is using those same locations when they go out—even if they are varying what they are doing—from the insurgent's perspective there is no variation. In other words, you may think you are varying your pattern, but if you aren't coordinating that with other units operating in the area, from the insurgent's perspective you are establishing a pattern. And so soon as they see a pattern they will take advantage of it. Their target is *us*, and when we adapt they adapt as well. (Allen, 2006)

The commander makes little or no distinction between the interests of his team and the interests of other teams. The commander only sees the "us" of the unit. His insights provide an important reminder of the importance of reflection on experience, since he starts his statement with the fact that the team's insights came from an after-action review. However, the review involved the team in the context of other teams. The commander's statement illustrates that coordinating action does not stop within the team but must occur among all the teams involved in achieving the same goal.

UNCOORDINATED ACTION

Compare the coordination of the highly effective military units with the coordination on Everest. Sandy Pittman posted this message on her website 5 days after the events:

The whole thing is like some kind of military strike, or war, or a car bomb or something. You go in with these plans, but then it hits. You hear rumors and don't know what really is going on. You listen to people around you and what they are experiencing but you're never sure what really is going on. And everything keeps changing. It takes days, maybe weeks or months, to piece it all together. (Outside Online, 1997)

Pittman notices the similarity of the actions taken on Everest to those of military teams. At the same time, the Everest teams failed to experience the effortless coordination that the combat teams achieved. In the Everest teams, people are "never sure what is going on." Only after days of piecing together the events do they become clear. In contrast, the combat teams made immediate sense of their environment through coordinated actions.

Pittman also posted an entry on her website that implied more interteam rivalry than coordination. She reported, "We are enthused, especially because (as far as we know) our team has made the most progress to date of any group climbing the mountain" (Pittman, 1996).

The Everest teams and the combat teams provide an important contrast for understanding goal pursuit. When teams members do not know what is going on, they are more likely to rely on their preconceived notion of how to act. In other words, they are more likely to continue to pursue a goal—to continue in the direction they were moving—even when a situation is confusing because pursuing the goal provides the most satisfying action. This is not to say that the combat situations described by Allen were orderly, but the combat leaders were able to make sense out of their situation more easily than the leaders on Everest. The combat teams displayed better ability to coordinate action because they learned to make sense of complex situations.

Minding the gap

One of the most pervasive issues confronting those who set and pursue challenging goals lies in differentiating between a goal to be achieved and a goal that has already been achieved. This seems a troubling issue, yet it lies at the heart of destructive goal pursuit. This occurrence—too close identification with an unachieved goal—appears to be a recurring phenomenon. The problem with this kind of goal-based identity is that it limits learning. It limits learning because it limits the kinds of information that the leader and the team consider and more importantly the kind of information they ignore. Because teams can become so entranced with their goals, they lose sight of the complexity and the challenges of the goal pursuit. Krakauer sums up the problem of goal identity:

> Unfortunately, the sort of individual who is programmed to ignore personal distress and keep pushing for the top is frequently programmed to disregard signs of grave and imminent danger as well. This forms the nub of a dilemma that every Everest climber eventually comes up against: in order to succeed you must be exceedingly driven, but if you're driven you're likely to die. Above 26,000 feet, moreover, the line between appropriate zeal and reckless summit fever becomes grievously thin. (Krakauer, 1997a, p. 177)

Goal identity may be tied to a certain type of individual, as Krakauer suggests, or it may be a social phenomenon. Either way, such a state does not have to be accepted. Climbers, like others who set and pursue high goals, face the dilemma of when to push forward and when to head back down. Failure to recognize the dilemma marks the first problem in commonly used approaches to goal-setting. Failure to recognize the dilemma of goal-setting can lead to the kinds of disasters experienced on Everest.

One mechanism to overcome such thin thinking rests in "minding the gap." This phrase comes from the London Underground system's pervasive warnings to "mind the gap" between the moving train and the railway platform. As stated in an earlier article, "Distracted passengers can easily become trapped between the station's platform and the allure of a fast-moving train. Like the promise of a fast-moving transport, the hasty achievement of goals can lure people into ignoring the gap between where one currently stands and what one hopes to achieve" (Kayes, 2005, p. 398).

Cultivating multiple goals

Researchers conducted a study to see if the nature of the task might impact the effectiveness of common goal-setting strategies (Earley, Connolly, and Ekegren, 1989). The study is described in more detail in Chapter 3. The researchers present three levels to consider when setting goals. Each of the three levels accounts for the type of task and the subsequent goal that should be set.

1. The first level of goal-setting focuses on the content of the task itself. Goal-setting works well when performance can be improved by increasing effort and energy, such as in situations that require manual work or simple production.
2. The second level involves a task that requires specific strategies to complete. Here, setting a specific and difficult goal works best because once you identify a single strategy, it tends to work well all the time.
3. At the third level, however, goal-setting goes awry. At this level, successful performance requires continued learning and the development of new strategies. Successful performance cannot be achieved from simple trial and error but only through detailed learning.

These findings confirm a belief long held by developmental psychologists such as Robert Kegan, Eric Erickson, and Abraham Maslow. Goal-setting is a complex process that requires not only constant re-evaluation, but also the ability to manage multiple, even conflicting, goals.

In summary, this chapter has outlined seven beliefs and behaviors that help leaders overcome the destructive pursuit of goals and realize the positive benefits of goal-setting and pursuit. When leaders face an ill-defined and unstructured problem, the normally helpful process of putting more effort into a course of action can be detrimental. These seven beliefs and behaviors emerge from improved teamwork and learning. Adopting these beliefs and behaviors will lead to a more complex understanding of the goal-setting process and, ultimately, to learning how to navigate dynamic problems.

Learning points

▶ Drawing from the Everest events, seven processes can be implemented to help teams avoid goalodicy: (1) recognizing ill-structured problems; (2) learning from experience; (3) engaging in recovery; (4) fostering trust; (5) developing tacit coordination; (6) minding the gap; and (7) cultivating multiple goals.

Learning questions

▶ How did the teams on Everest display or not display each of these processes? Is any particular process more or less important in determining the effectiveness of the group? Why or why not?
▶ Think of a team you are on or have been a part of in the past. Did any of these processes exist in your team?
▶ Think back to the previous chapter on leadership. How can leaders foster the seven processes that forestall goalodicy? How can leaders help teams achieve higher levels of goal-setting?

Part IV Rethinking Leadership in Organizations

10   Rethinking Leadership in Organizations

This chapter argues that scholars and practitioners alike spend too much time thinking about goals and not enough time thinking about learning. This emphasis on goals at the expense of learning is particularly troublesome in the area of leadership. Conventional wisdom on leadership suggests that leaders should set ambitious and challenging goals and then get out of the way (e.g., Hackman, 2002). This chapter suggests that this kind of thinking can lead to disastrous consequences because it assumes too much from both teams and leaders.

Another approach is to learn from organizations involved in risky situations. These organizations are often called *high-reliability organizations* because they must function well at all times or fall into disaster. A better understanding of high-reliability organizations shows the limits of putting too much faith or responsibility in one leader. The chapter takes lessons from the rescue attempt on Everest to learn about leadership and also includes examples of effective leadership found in the Blackfoot Indians of North America and airline cockpit crews. These examples demonstrate a process called reciprocal leadership, which defines leadership from the perspective of coordination among team members.

A better understanding of how to move from destructive to productive pursuit of goals begins with questioning conventional wisdom about the nature of leadership in the goal-setting process. In the chapters leading up to this point, the book has argued that leaders on Everest sought to take a hard line about the actions of their team members and failed to develop their team members. The lack of team and individual development meant that many of the team members could not respond to ill-defined problems. Leaders Fischer and Hall seemed to embrace a conventional form of leadership. Even though both leaders had relatively different styles in terms of personality and direction, Fischer and Hall shared some conventional wisdom regarding what was necessary for the teams to accomplish their goals.

Leadership and goals: Conventional wisdom

Conventional wisdom about leading goal-directed behavior can be seen in the following advice given to leaders by well-known researcher Richard Hackman (2002) at Harvard University:

> To foster self-managing, goal-directed work, those who create work teams should be insistent and unapologetic about exercising their authority to specify end states, but equally insistent about *not* specifying the details of the means by which the team is to pursue those ends. (p. 73; emphasis in original)

This thinking leads to problems. Hackman states that the goals need to be specified but the means to achieve the goals should not be specified. The statement reflects a fundamental misunderstanding of team learning and the goal-setting process. When leaders begin to specify end states at the expense of providing appropriate strategies, the goal-setting process begins to break down. Yes, leaders need to help specify end states, but more importantly, leaders need to provide support to help teams achieve these end states by facilitating learning within the team. Conventional wisdom, as represented by Hackman's statement, breaks down because it depends too much on the leadership and too much on goals. This kind of thinking is detrimental to teamwork because it emphasizes goals at the expense of learning in teams.

Current thinking on goals is limited because it assumes that the person in the leadership role is capable of setting and leading the pursuit of goals. As the actions of the leaders on Everest indicate, leaders may hold the technical skills to complete a task, but they often fail at being able to manage the difficult and challenging psychological dynamics that emerge in teams. Previous chapters have outlined some of these complex dynamics. For example, dependence on the leader, the emergence of competing demands, and the inability to develop a shared goal structure are some of the elements of complex team dynamics. Traditional approaches to setting and pursuing challenging goals may work well when a situation is simple and predefined. Putting leaders in charge of goals but not in a place to assist climbers leads to problems when situations become more complex and can result in unintended consequences of goal pursuit.

The continued effort to reach the Everest summit by exhausted climbers resulted in unintended consequences because the climbers were not psychologically well equipped for the climb. Leaders Fischer and Hall themselves became trapped on the summit by helping climbers down late in the afternoon. At first, the typical dependency on leaders continued.

Beidleman, Fischer's assistant guide, led a small group of climbers that remained on the summit for over an hour as they waited for Fischer to give the okay to descend. Hall was now devoting his time exclusively to Doug Hansen, who was struggling to get to the top and becoming weaker by the minute. Assistant guide Boukreev had chosen to climb alone, without bottled oxygen, and had already begun his descent to Camp IV without any clients in tow. Jangbu, also an assistant to Fischer, continued to assist Pittman up the mountain. Other climbers, more experienced perhaps or even stronger, or just more willing to go at it alone, pursued the summit without direction from leadership. Beck Weathers remained stranded, shivering alone in the cold for hours waiting for Hall to return.

At this point, team members could no longer rely solely on their leaders if they hoped to survive. The leaders and their followers became exhausted by their pursuit of the summit and failed to reserve enough energy to get back down. The leaders became stretched to their limit, incapable of managing the growing complexity of the situation. Unable to meet all the demands they faced, the leadership in the groups began to fall apart. For the next few hours, climbers faced being trapped on the mountain. Learning and teamwork provided the only way down.

Leadership and goalodicy

The problem with conventional wisdom about the role of leaders in the goal-setting process is that it focuses mainly on the external content of goal-setting and fails to account for the coordinated behavior that occurs during teamwork. If we want to understand the role of the leader, we need to begin to look at the internal processes that drive leaders and their followers to develop, pursue, and maintain goals. Only when we understand the internal nature of the goal-setting process, as opposed to the external structure of goals, can we understand why leaders engage in destructive goal pursuit.

Setting and pursuing goals is an emotional process, but it is not enough to say that the destructive pursuit of goals is irrational or arbitrary. Destructive goal pursuit rests on an internal logic of its own, but in order to understand this logic, we cannot simply look at goal-setting; we need to search for how leaders use information in the pursuit of goals. Everest teams provide an important source of data in this search because action teams intensify the need for information, especially when a team is directly engaged in the expedition. As a group of researchers noted, "Action teams need [communication] systems that can rapidly deliver task-critical information about fast-changing, situation-driven events in real time" (Bikson, Cohen, and Mankin, 1999, p. 232).

The first thing necessary in a search for a better explanation of leadership is a better understanding of how leaders understand and filter the information they have available to them. Once we understand the nature of how leaders learn, then we can begin to decipher goal-setting from the perspective of the leader. How does the leader understand the situation that he or she faces? This look inside the leader focuses on how leaders conceive of their commitment to goals and how they justify the continued pursuit of goals in the face of contradictory evidence. Only when we understand the perspective of the leader can we answer the primary question posed in this book: *Why would a climber continue to pursue the summit of the mountain despite evidence he could not make it down safely?*

Leadership requires rallying individuals around a common goal, creating a clear and compelling vision of the future. Molly and Marshall Sashkin (2003), two of the world's top authorities on visionary leadership, take the prospects of goal-setting even further to suggest that leadership and followership is defined by the future vision that a leader creates. If it is true that leadership requires vision and goal-setting, then how leaders justify and pursue goals provides important data for understanding leadership. In addition, how leaders enlist followers into the vision and use goals to promote followership is critical. A significant question is, when does vision become productive and when does it become destructive for both leaders and followers?

Beyond conventional leadership: Reciprocal leadership

One thing seems certain: to meet the demands required of leadership in high-intensity situations, leaders need to manage competing goals. Leadership requires taking action, but leadership also requires developing individual members so that each member can take on a leadership role to accomplish different goals. Leadership needs to change hands within a team, not be confined to one individual. This back-and-forth play between leadership responsibilities can be called *reciprocal leadership*. The term *reciprocal* comes from a well-known model of task design that suggests that tasks require group members to continually pass information back and forth in order to complete the task or shift roles as this information is transformed.

Think, for example, about the difference between basketball and golf. In basketball, each member of the team plays a different role: one team member may be a good shooter, another member a good ball handler, and yet another member good at rebounding the ball. Taken separately, not one of these roles is sufficient for the team to successfully reach a goal. However, when a team combines roles, the basketball moves back and forth between team members, and each member assumes leadership for his or her own role.

Contrast the basketball team with a game of golf. Players are responsible for hitting their own ball and tracking their own score. Even in the clever games of golf designed to be team games, where players rotate turns or play where the best ball lay on the course, there is little or no coordination between team members. Each member is responsible for the ultimate success of his or her own shot, even if the scores are kept collectively. The difference between basketball and golf is not just in the skill of team members; the difference is in the nature of the coordination among members. Leadership is not just about the skills of individual team members doing their best, but in the way that the leadership responsibilities are handed over between individuals.

The argument here is that leadership needs to look more like the reciprocal interdependence of the basketball team. When leadership emerges from reciprocal interdependence, individual performance becomes enhanced, and individuals can perform at an even higher level as they draw on the strengths of and coordinate with other members. When leadership is reciprocal, the burdens of leadership lie as much among individuals as within them. No individual has exclusive control of leadership for any sustained period or for any entire team task.

RECIPROCAL LEADERSHIP IN THE BLACKFOOT INDIANS

The great humanist psychologist Abraham Maslow (1998) noticed this kind of reciprocal leadership when observing Blackfoot Indian chiefs of North America. He called attention to four characteristics of their leadership. First, instead of relying on general leaders, the chiefs relied on the coordination of several individual, or specialist, leaders to guide the group through particular situations, such as waging war, raising stock, managing political diplomacy, or coordinating special ceremonies. Second, the group members were realistic about the leader's talents. This meant that the Blackfoot believe that a leader was the one person best suited for the particular job. Being realistic about the leadership capacity of the individual also meant that the tribe recognized limitations. They knew that an individual good at leading one task may not be as good when leading other tasks. A leader in one situation might be the last in line for another. Third, the leaders did not command authority or even issue orders; rather, leadership was enacted through cues and signals that were used to pattern and organize group actions. These cues remained in place for long periods of time and were understood by all parties in the group. Fourth, the leadership role was only temporary. Leadership was never invested in one individual for any period of time but was based on particular circumstances and demands. When there was no need for a leader, the leadership simply went away and the tribes functioned effectively without clear leadership (pp. 153–154).

RECIPROCAL LEADERSHIP IN THE RESCUE ON EVEREST

The Everest teams began to look like the Blackfoot Indians during their descent of the mountain. Hall and Fischer led many of the climbers to the summit, but it was the reciprocal interactions of climbers that led them down to safety. As the Everest team leaders Hall, Fischer, and Gau struggled for their survival, two collections of climbers began to organize themselves in order to remain alive. Had the teams continued to rely on Hall and Fischer to get down the mountain, members may have become trapped along with their leaders at some unreachable point on the mountain.

The reciprocity among Neil Beidleman, Klev Schoening, Mike Groom, Anatoli Boukreev, and others led one group of climbers to safety at Camp IV. Then it was the reciprocal interactions of climbers from other expeditions like Pete Athans, Todd Burleson, Ed Viesturs, and David Breashears that led the surviving climbers down to lower camps.

For example, the newly formed team consisting of Beidleman, Groom, Schoening, Weathers, Pittman, Fox, and Madsen became lost in the storm. The team huddled together to form a human barrier against the wind, which had reached a speed of 70 miles an hour. In a literal fight to keep their bodies from freezing, the climbers rubbed and pounded each other's muscles and shouted at each other to stay awake. Falling asleep at that altitude and in that temperature foretells death. After several hours in the huddle, assistant guides Beidleman and Groom spotted a clearing in the clouds and identified the Big Dipper. They then relied on the stars to navigate their way back to Camp IV, which they now realized was just a few hundred yards from the huddle. Both collapsed from exhaustion upon reaching the camp, but not before directing Boukreev, who had rested now for several hours, to the stranded climbers. At first, Boukreev could not find the climbers, but he persisted until he literally dragged Pittman, Madsen, and Fox the several hundred yards to Camp IV.

Leadership passed among the members. The teams engaged in a number of different activities: navigating, encouraging, orienting, huddling, carrying, and directing. None of these skills was exclusive to any one individual, although some individuals displayed more than one skill. Rather, these skills were represented by a collectivity of leadership skills.

The rescuers again displayed reciprocal leadership in the final movement of injured climbers off the mountain. When Pete Athans and Todd Burleson were at Camp III and heard of the developing problems at Camp IV, they abandoned their own summit attempt and headed up the mountain. The next morning, May 11, they found the ailing climbers alone and without help. Some of the climbers had already begun to descend to safer altitude, leaving those too weak to continue down at Camp V. Athans and Burleson, two of the most experienced climbers on Everest, described the situation as a war zone. As soon as they arrived, they began delivering oxygen to the tents of ailing climbers as if they were delivering pizzas (Coburn, 1997). At the same time, a climbing team consisting of veteran climbers Ed Viesturs and David Breashears, who were on Everest to film an IMAX large-format movie, began to organize a rescue effort from their position lower on the mountain.

One group of Sherpas had organized a search party to reach Fischer and Gau but were unable to rouse Fischer. Short-roping Gau behind them, a difficult and dangerous act at high altitude, the strong climbers returned to Camp IV with Gau in tow. Boukreev defied the advice of experienced climbers and set out to find Fischer, realizing, only after he had risked his own life once again, that he could not revive the nearly dead Fischer. For his efforts, Boukreev was awarded the highest honor by the American Alpine Club.

Once the climbers arrived at Camp I, just above the ice fall, all was still not well. Unable to carry the ailing Weathers and Gau down through the treacherous icefall that separated Camp I from base camp, the team began to lose hope because no helicopter had ever successfully landed above the icefall. It looked like the climbers would die there. The lives of these men relied on the reciprocal leadership of yet another makeshift team. Nepali helicopter pilot Madan K. C. flew from the city of Katmandu to the encampment at nearly 20,000 feet, something never before attempted. Guided by a makeshift landing strip marked by pink Kool-Aid, Madan lifted Gau to a lower camp and returned in about 45 minutes to airlift Weathers, who was still struggling with frostbite and extreme exhaustion. Weathers gave up his spot on the helicopter to Gau, who was in worse condition.

The rescue of Weathers and Gau represented a variety of leadership skills, each of which required the coordination of multiple kinds of expertise and competence. Again, the survival of team members lay not in the head or hands of any single leader. In particular, the lives of the members no longer rested in the designated group leaders, who had been severed from the group days earlier. Rather, survival was embedded in the reciprocal interdependence of the leadership that remained in the ad hoc rescue team.

Reciprocal leadership and teamwork in high-reliability organizations

Developing reciprocal leadership in teams requires an understanding that a team goal, even one as seemingly individual as mountain climbing, is based upon interdependence of leadership. Interdependence of leadership can be seen in this statement by experienced Himalayan guide Jim Williams:

> It's important to realize that everybody's on that mountain... no matter whose team you're on. That eventually you need to lend assistance as it becomes necessary. I don't think... there's really much room for sort of staying isolated and not lending assistance. (Outside Online, 1997, p. 6)

Expeditions provide one example of a high-reliability group because they face an ill-structured task and because the consequences of failure are great. Other high-reliability organizations include nuclear power plants, chemical storage and manufacturing facilities, and airliners. One key distinguishing characteristic of high-reliability organizations is that they cannot experience the normal breakdowns faced by other organizations. The consequences of a breakdown are much too great. High-reliability organizations must be designed for resilience, and those organizations must respond to even minor problems with immediate and decisive intervention. Otherwise, the consequences would be fatal. Weick and his colleagues argue that all organizations, even those engaged in the most mundane and inconsequential of activities, can learn from these high-reliability organizations (Weick, Sutcliffe, and Obstfeld, 1999).

Airplane cockpit crews have been studied extensively and provide insight into some strengths and weaknesses of high-reliability organizations. After the introduction of jet-propelled engines on commercial aircraft, a study conducted by the National Aeronautics and Space Administration revealed some interesting, if troubling, news. More than 70 percent of airline accidents were related, in some way or another, to a failure in teamwork. Even when the equipment itself failed, that failure was likely accompanied by a related breakdown in human interaction (Helmreich, 1997). Current evidence accumulated by the National Transportation Safety Board, the U.S. government agency responsible for conducting independent evaluations of airliner accidents, seems to support the same conclusion. Nearly 90 percent of all airline accidents involve human breakdowns of some kind. What is interesting about these findings for the discussion of leadership is that they suggest that most breakdowns in leadership arise from teamwork issues, not from either task-related issues or even individual cognitive breakdowns. Needless to say, eliminating some of the problems of teamwork in the cockpit has been a key area of interest for both the airline industry and regulators.

Robert Ginnett (1990) (see also Hackman, 2002; Weiner, Kanki, and Helmreich, 1995) has spent a good deal of time analyzing how leadership affects the effectiveness of cockpit crews. In one study, Ginnett identified three behaviors displayed by crew captains who were perceived as superior by expert pilots. First, the top leaders established their legitimacy by what they already knew. This is no surprise: everyone expects leaders to be experts in their field. But the top leaders also made clear what they did not know and in what areas they required more information. Second, the leaders established boundaries. The best leaders did not interact only with the cockpit crew but considered all members of the flight team, including the cabin crew, as part of the team. Third, the top captains established an environment of interaction. This meant that the captain not only set the tone for the task, but also established the tone for how individuals would speak to one another.

The best cockpit crew captains create shared beliefs among team members of inclusion, trust, and open communication. These shared beliefs are crucial for successful teamwork in action teams because they facilitate knowledge sharing among team members. While the best captains clarified the hierarchy, they also created an environment for effective teamwork by allowing others to engage in the situation openly.

DEVELOPING COORDINATION IN LEADERS

Chapters 8 and 9 showed how many teams work together seamlessly, with members anticipating the behaviors and beliefs of their teammates. This process, called tacit coordination, presents one of the ways teams accomplish goals. Teams that demonstrate tacit coordination demonstrate a level of team competency that suggests they are on the right track to accomplishing their task. Tacit coordination is one indicator of team learning.

Team leaders can foster team learning behavior such as tacit coordination through two mechanisms. One method rests in putting together intact teams that train and work together to respond to problems. Some teams, such as firefighters, special forces teams, and special police units, train together in the same unit that will eventually carry out the task.

Training together as a team allows teams to improve synchronization and adjustment, the kinds of tacit coordination skills essential for team performance outcomes. Other teams such as commercial airline cockpit crews, wildland firefighters, surgery teams, and some emergency response teams often change team membership from activity to activity. For example, airline cockpit crews often change with each flight. Each time a plane prepares for take-off, a new team is formed in the cockpit and remains intact for the duration of the flight. A team's lifecycle is bound by a single take-off and landing. Despite the fact that cockpit crews form and reform thousands of times a day throughout the world, these action team are some of the most effective and reliable teams that can be found.

The constant forming and reforming of cockpit crews provides us with an important lesson. Just because team members do not know each other does not mean that the team will fail in coordination. Airline cockpit crews overcome the potential for problems in coordination by receiving extensive individual training in procedures and rules prior to joining a team. Pilots know procedures well, such as how to carry out a preflight checklist and standardized rules governing take-offs and landings. To state the obvious, pilots also know the mechanics of how to fly a plane.

By developing standardized procedures, individual team members are more likely to share expectations and a common response pattern to problems. Intensive individual training also serves another purpose. It facilitates a culture of shared beliefs and values. Among mountain climbers, for example, a shared ethic exists about helping other team members. The shared beliefs are based on self-reliance and team interdependence. This seemingly contradictory ethic can be maintained only by a strong system of shared beliefs among climbers. The shared beliefs serve to set expectations, maintain an orderly system, and foster trust that team members will do what they can to support other members. These shared beliefs support the coordinating behaviors so characteristic of teamwork.

Notice that the 1996 Mt Everest teams did not seem to share many of the beliefs believed to be important for effective teamwork. Unlike commercial airline pilots who receive extensive training in procedures, the Everest teams received no extensive individual training on "proper" procedures. The lack of training is evident in the lack of understanding that team members had about one of the most crucial elements of the climb—turnaround times. Other accounts point to general ignorance of basic procedures, such as how and when to strap climbing crampons on boots.

Extensive individual training in procedures, like those received by airline pilots, may not have mattered on Everest if the teams had trained together for an extensive period of time as they prepared for the summit attempt. Unlike expeditions in the past, where individual climbers had several days, weeks, or even months of shared time together, the 1996 Mt Everest teams spent about 21 days together—and much of that time did not involve working as a team. In contrast, the 1963 AMEE team spent nearly 100 days together. The difference in time spent together as a team is not in and of itself the main issue; more important is the relationships and sense of shared trust that develop over time when people work together as a team. For example, the anthropologist Von Furer-Haimendorf (1984) lamented the changing relationship between Sherpa guides and their western clients:

> Previously, western visitors to Nepal, whether they were mountaineers, explorers or anthropologists, lived for months at close quarters with individual Sherpas, and often maintained a relationship which extended over a number of journeys and even several years. Hence close ties of friendship were established and neither partner considered their cooperation as a mere business relationship. Now Sherpas employed by a trekking agency or working freelance from bases in Katmandu, accompany one anonymous group of tourists after the other, and there is no time for the growth of any feelings of mutual understanding or loyalty. (p. 68)

This comment could easily reflect the changing relationship among climbers on Everest—who no longer shared the same sense of loyalty and understanding either with other western climbers or with Sherpa guides. Even though climbers and guides may be bound by the "dangers and triumphs" (p. 68) of mountaineering, this shared sense of purpose failed to exist in many of the individuals climbing Everest in 1996. Without a shared sense of purpose and loyalty, it was difficult to develop any type of coordination among group members.

Learning in high-reliability organizations

Action remains the core attribute studied in leadership. What leaders do, rather than how they think or what they know, seems to be the focus. Most leadership development programs focus on teaching leaders how to act, not how to think. The emphasis in these programs lies in helping leaders to act in tricky situations. The Everest events reveal that leading requires thinking as much as acting, recognizing consequences as much as setting goals. What leaders know (or, for that matter, what leaders fail to notice) provides an additional focus for leadership development training. This was the conclusion reached by one group of psychologists. After spending countless hours studying how organizations can best respond to change, they suggested that leaders need to develop the wisdom of learning (Weick, Sutcliffe, and Obstfeld, 1999).

One of the most intriguing conclusions Weick and his colleagues make is that learning is defined not so much by the direct behavior of those in the organization, but by what kind of information the organization ignores (p. 95). It is within these gaps, or ignorance, that we begin to understand how these organizations respond to problems. This same logic of ignorance can help us understand the role of leadership. What if leadership were defined not by the kinds of behaviors of the leader, but rather by what kinds of information the leader ignored?

LEARNING DEFINED BY WHAT LEADERS IGNORE

Focusing on what leaders ignore rather than on how they behave puts a slightly different spin on leadership. It involves moving away from judging leaders by their behaviors, such as their ability to inspire or motivate, or by their personal characteristics, such as their charisma or ability to use power to persuade and direct, and instead focusing on how they learn. When leaders ignore information that may be valuable, they are making statements about what they learn. The Everest teams ignored information a number of times:

▶ Pittman (1996) and Beidleman (in Boukreev and DeWalt, 1997) minimized the importance of increasingly painful coughs, stating that they were necessary discomforts of high altitude.
▶ Weathers became blind during his ascent and was unable to see even a few feet in front of him. The blindness arose as an unintended side effect of the corrective eye surgery he had had a few years earlier. Weathers believed his vision would improve as he approached the summit and the warmth of the sun (Coburn, 1997; Krakauer, 1997a).
▶ Weathers further commented: "Fortunately, I didn't really need to see the route, because deep steps had been kicked ahead of me" (Coburn, 1997, p. 178).
▶ Lopsang Jangbu—who was vomiting near the summit, a sign of altitude sickness—stated that vomiting was his body's normal reaction to high altitude (Jangbu, 1996).
▶ Leader Fischer wrote off increasingly weak and sick team members by claiming "it's attitude not altitude."
▶ The day before the summit, Fischer carried down an ailing climber, returning 8 hours later. Also, Fischer was believed to be suffering from an illness that caused fatigue. He chose to ignore these weaknesses on summit day as just "dragging ass."

▶ Team leaders laughed off suggestions by Sherpa guides that the climbers were not taking the climb seriously enough. Although the Sherpas collectively have more experience than any climbing team, their views were seen as "superstition."

▶ Most important of all, climbers ignored the pre-established turnaround times and continued for the summit, despite increasing evidence the summit could not be reached safely.

These and other examples show some of the gaps that began to emerge between expectation and experience. The gap between what is expected (e.g., goals) and what is experienced (e.g., data) provides an opening that may tempt leaders to engage in the destructive pursuit of goals. As the gap between the desired goal and the immediate experience widens, leaders can either choose to learn or choose to reinforce existing beliefs.

Recall the 1963 American Everest Expedition described in Chapter 2. Detailed analysis of the climbers' conversations as well as a reading of their personal climbing journals revealed that the teams tended to create information that contradicted what was experienced in their environment. For example, if the weather looked promisingly pleasant, the teams would consider that the weather might change for the worse. When the teams considered the possibility of reaching the summit using the new western route, they consistently underestimated their chances at success. In both cases, the teams appeared to see the worst-case scenario and filtered positive indicators in favor of negative indicators of success.

On the one hand, the teams were reinforcing their existing belief that the goals would be difficult to achieve. Thus, the teams kept focused on their goal. The more the team strived for the goal, the more the team sought information that increased uncertainty about achieving the goal. The increased uncertainty led the teams to invest more energy into achieving the goal. On the other hand, the team's continued search for contradictory information also served another purpose: it kept learning alive. Learning continued to occur in these climbing teams because the discrepancies between the goal and the experience were kept distinct. In the language introduced in Chapter 9, these teams continued to "mind the gap" between idealized vision and current circumstances. In the end, the strategy proved successful, as six climbers from the 1963 expedition reached the summit by two different routes. The expedition was not without the loss of many toes to frostbite. Since that successful and historic summit, only six teams have reached the summit via the difficult western route in over 40 attempts, resulting in at least 23 deaths.

In contrast, the 1996 Everest expeditions appeared to close the gap between vision and experience. The difference between the 1963 expedition and the 1996 expedition rested not in factors such as the commercial nature of the two expeditions, the personalities of the climbers or leaders, or the economic relationships between the climbers and leaders. Indeed, the teams did not even seem to be that different in their desire or effort to reach the summit. In other words, there appears to be little difference in either their goals or their goal pursuit. All these expeditions appeared to reinforce goals through the information they acquired. The difference between the 1996 and the 1963 expeditions comes down to the following. The 1963 teams developed the ability to learn in the face of challenging goals and the wisdom of recognizing what is not known.

THE WISDOM OF "NOT KNOWING"

To say that leadership is to be judged by what is ignored is to suggest that leaders embrace the wisdom of "not knowing." Eleanor Duckworth (1996), a student of the famous child psychologist Jean Piaget, describes the wisdom of not knowing as being able to take advantage of opportunities for learning. Taking advantage of these opportunities requires "accepting surprise, puzzlement, excitement, patience, caution, honest attempts and wrong outcomes as legitimate" (p. 69; cited in Kayes, 2002a, p. 197).

Leaders of all sorts should recognize the need to change course in the face of changes. Robert McNamara, a successful business executive, held several important business leadership posts at Ford Motors and later served as head of the World Bank. Of all the successes McNamara achieved, however, he is most remembered by the limits of his leadership. McNamara assumed the head of the U.S. Department of Defense during the Vietnam crisis. By his own admittance, he failed to see factors that were not part of the initial equation. One reason McNamara wore blinders during much of the crisis could be found in his work at Ford. McNamara believed, as do most business leaders, that all key factors were known. This may have certainly been true at Ford. When McNamara was at the helm of Ford, building and selling automobiles was a systematic, step-by-step process, a perfect situation for setting and pursuing challenging goals. Conducting a military police action abroad, however, was based on a different set of factors, many of them unknown and many of them changing regularly. McNamara failed to consider that factors that were not included in the initial calculations could be important. He failed to heed the advice of top military aides and others closer to the situation who saw discrepancies between goals and experiences. What McNamara and other top aides failed to see, what they ignored, resulted in tens of thousands of military and civilian deaths (as recounted in Bennis and O'Toole, 2005).

Missing key factors is not a limitation preserved for business or military leaders, although those in business may be particularly vulnerable— because of the value the business world places on rational analysis and the training business professionals undergo. Warren Bennis, one of the early thinkers on group dynamics and a well-known scholar, made this claim along with his colleague James O'Toole and argues that the current training of leaders depends too much on traditional analysis at the expense of understanding the human side of leadership.

Howard Gardner, a psychologist and recipient of the MacArthur "genius" award, has made a similar pronouncement about selecting, being attentive to, and processing information and its importance for leadership (Gardner, 2006). Gardner seems to imply, however, that this task is locked in the head of the individual rather than in the cooperation among individuals. The idea of reciprocal leadership can be distinguished from the standpoint of Gardner and others because it focuses on the need to rely on others to understand information. One lesson we can learn from Hall and Fischer is that leaders who isolate themselves too much from the rest of the team fail to learn and ultimately stumble.

Learning points

▶ Conventional wisdom on leadership says that leaders should set high and ambitious goals and let teams figure out on their own how to achieve those goals. This position fails to recognize the importance of developing followers as an essential task of leadership.
▶ An alternative model of leadership is put forth based on reciprocity among team members. Reciprocal leadership describes how teams coordinate and pass leadership responsibilities between members.
▶ Expeditions and airline cockpit crews provide examples of high-reliability organizations that require learning in order to respond to novel situations. The examples illustrate that what is ignored can be more important to leadership than what leaders actually do.

Learning questions

▶ How is reciprocal leadership different than other kinds of leadership? Using the Everest case as well as your own experience, think of some examples of reciprocal leadership. Under what conditions might reciprocal leadership not be effective?
▶ How can leaders develop a better sense of the situation they face so they are less likely to ignore important data? How might you instruct

future guides or clients on Everest to look for important clues to what they might face?
▶ Think about your own team or organization. What are some of the issues or events that would make your organization vulnerable to disaster? What are some of the most important things you can do to prevent these things from happening? What specific steps can you take to overcome them? What information are you and your team or organization currently ignoring?

11 Conclusion: Putting Leadership into Action

Goals shape the future by creating a vision of what can be achieved. But when goals become the sole driver for action, destructive goal pursuit begins to take shape. The 1996 Mt Everest climbing disaster, in particular the teams led by Scott Fischer and Rob Hall, provides a compelling illustration of the process of destructive goal pursuit. As the climbers continued to put more and more effort into reaching the summit and continued to ignore pre-established turnaround times, the team of climbers pursued the summit at the cost of their own lives.

The actions of these teams illustrate the paradox of goals: setting challenging and ambitious goals compels us to reach new heights and achieve greater success, but failure to abandon some goals can lead to disastrous consequences. Pursuit of goals can lead to the exact opposite of what one initially hoped to achieve. The irony of the Everest disaster lies in the fact that most of the climbers from both teams actually achieved the summit. How does one make sense of a goal that can be achieved only by sacrificing one's life?

This book provides an explanation of why the Everest teams continued to pursue the summit in face of evidence it could not be safely attained. The line of thinking pursued in this book suggests that there is something inherent in the goal-setting process itself that can lead to dysfunctional goal pursuit. This hidden source of vulnerability remains mostly ignored by scholars and sidestepped by leaders.

And there is good reason to ignore the unintended consequences inherent in the goal-setting process. Leaders seem to ignore the limits of goal-setting because goal-setting serves an important purpose—to rally followers around an appealing, if idealized, vision of the future. Without setting goals, leaders may think there is little left to do to create a common direction for followers. To abandon this vision is often as dramatic as abandoning one's own identity and worth as a leader.

Scholars too have embraced goal-setting as a kind of all-encompassing approach to motivation. Goal-setting remains one of the most influential and widely studied behaviors in organizational studies. The almost religious status achieved by goal-setting as a practice makes it both an easy target and a difficult one to challenge. Goal-setting is an easy target because it has been studied so extensively that flaws and holes are bound

167

to emerge under such scrutiny. At the same time, goal-setting is difficult to challenge because questioning its efficacy is like challenging a religious canon. Since the evidence for the effectiveness of goal-setting remains so compelling, scholars have been reluctant to find fault. Instead, scholars have chosen to rationalize away contradictory findings and ignore disconfirming evidence that exposes the limits of goal-setting. The analogy should become clear. Just as the Everest teams continued to ignore data that challenged their belief that they could achieve a goal, so scholars ignore some of the evidence that challenges their belief in goal-setting.

With the limitations of leadership in the forefront, this book has set out to find an explanation for the 1996 Mt Everest climbing disaster that goes broader and deeper than many of the explanations offered by the press, existing psychology, and even the theories put forth by survivors and experts on climbing. Surely, many of the factors suggested by these observers and participants played a role in the disaster. Ambitious but inexperienced climbers, changing obligations between guides and clients, lack of teamwork, the effects of altitude, and the sheer number of climbers on the mountain that season all must have played a role.

This book reveals another explanation: the problem of goalodicy, destructive goal pursuit. Goalodicy exposes how goal-setting itself may have contributed to the disaster. The source of the problem may have begun even before the leaders and followers arrived on Everest, as the narrow goal of reaching the summit already merged with the identity of the climbers. Follower dependence on the leaders fueled destructive goal pursuit as climbers put faith in their leaders to help them achieve individual goals. Such dependence may have been fine under other conditions, but in 1996, the leaders were taxed beyond their limits. The leaders struggled for their own lives alongside followers.

The climbers may have become overwhelmed by the situation, but they failed to recognize the destructiveness of their own pursuit. The climbers had the goal of reaching the summit in mind, and now reaching the summit was in sight. While some climbers chose to abandon their bid for the summit or simply collapsed under the pressure, members of Fischer's and Hall's teams remained determined to reach the summit. Bruce Herrod, the ailing climber from the South African team, failed to heed the warning signs as well. In unwavering pursuit of the summit, these climbers provide all too much insight into the largely ignored phenomenon of destructive goal pursuit.

Fortunately, the story continues beyond the deaths of the 15 climbers who died on Everest that season and even beyond the eight that died from the two expeditions. The struggle of the remaining climbers and the support of experienced and prudent climbers from other teams ensued, providing lessons for how to recover from destructive goal pursuit or avoid its dangers from the start. The coordinated efforts of teams spread up and down the mountain, across the country and even the world, secured the lives of those who remained.

The rescue efforts show that if it was the unwavering pursuit of the summit that ultimately stranded climbers on the mountain, it was learning from each other that ultimately got them back down. The efforts to save the climbers on Everest remain one of the most compelling stories of team learning that can be found. The coordinated efforts of rescuers should provide comfort to those who have become weary of the redemptive power of goals and goal-setting. The rescue efforts provide an alternative route to achievement. This alternative involves teamwork, learning, and reciprocal leadership. Just as goals get people into problems, learning provides a way out.

Also, as the book has shown, no one can be comfortable with learning as a goal in and of itself. Learning is a complex process, replete with challenges, setbacks, and problems of its own. Simply setting out to "learn" as a goal may increase effort, but it says nothing about the skills, knowledge, or abilities necessary to reach that goal.

Everest and the contemporary organization

For those still questioning what they can learn from Everest that may apply to their own organization, Table 5 provides a laundry list of characteristics that describe the nature of the contemporary organization. The list comes from comprehensive observations of how organizations have changed in the last quarter century (e.g., see Lawrence, 1987). The list provides further evidence that what climbers experienced on Everest may be strikingly similar to the challenges faced by many organizations.

The 1996 Mt Everest climbing disaster provides an important source of learning, not just for leaders of action-driven teams like those on Everest, but for leaders at all times. The events illustrate not only the problem of goalodicy but also the way to achieve goals in a more reasonable way.

In the final analysis, the events provide an uneasy message: setting and pursuing difficult goals works, but goals are always achieved at a price. Ultimately, it is not the goals that lead to disaster but ignoring the signs of destructive goal pursuit. Decades of research and practice on goal-setting show us that goals can facilitate the achievement of new heights because they increase effort toward the goal. The Everest events show how the same mechanisms that lead to goal achievement may also lead to failure. When achieving an outcome requires increased effort, goals work. When the means to achieving an outcome is unclear, goals may facilitate disaster.

Table 5 **Everest and the contemporary organization**

Characteristic	Present in high-altitude teams on Everest	Present in contemporary organizations
Pressure to achieve continually higher goals	✓	✓
Increased use of rigid outcome performance criteria	✓	✓
Greater interorganizational competition	✓	✓
Declining value of long-term relationships with employees	✓	✓
Action orientation	✓	✓
Drive toward short-term performance	✓	✓
Reliance on short-term project teams such as task forces and ad hoc teams to carry out tasks	✓	✓
Ability of individual actions to affect team or organizational outcomes	✓	✓
Multicultural environment	✓	✓
Coordination of work spanning time and space	✓	✓
Unpredictable, even hostile environment	✓	✓
Placement of personal goals before organizational goals	✓	✓
Participants' alienation from organizations	✓	✓

As long as goals fuel the pursuit of an idealized future, leaders will continue to pursue goals as yet unachieved. Destructive goal pursuit is likely to remain a problem not just in high-risk activities like mountain climbing, but in pursuits both lofty and modest. As the actions of leaders reach farther and take on greater consequence, destructive goal pursuit becomes a problem too important to ignore. Learning and knowledge deserve as much attention as blind pursuit of idealized goals.

Note on Method

This analysis use primary and secondary source archival data. When possible, the analysis relied on primary accounts of survivors and participants to piece together the events. Many of these primary sources were in the form of published book length memoirs, Internet postings, and televised interviews by survivors. In some cases, secondary sources were used such as reports, stories from newspapers and television. For a more detailed account of methodology, including issues of reliability of this account, see Kayes (2004a).

References

ABC News. (1996a, June 2). Mountain madness [segment of *60 Minutes*]. Michael Rosenbaum, Producer. New York: ABC.

ABC News. (1996b, September 16). Mountain without mercy: The Mt. Everest story [segment of *Turning Point*]. Betsy West, Executive Producer. New York: ABC News.

Allen, N. (2006). *Leaders in Iraq* [unpublished manuscript]. Washington, DC: The George Washington University and The United States Military Academy.

Ancona, D. G. and Caldwell, D. F. (1992). Bridging the boundary: External activity and performance in organizational teams. *Administrative Science Quarterly, 37*(4), 634–665.

Audia, P. G., Locke, E. A., and Smith, K. A. (2000). The paradox of success: An archival and laboratory study of strategic persistence following radical environmental change. *Academy of Management Journal, 34*(5), 837–853.

Baker, A. C., Jensen, P. J., and Kolb, D. A. (2002). *Conversational Learning: An Experiential Approach to Knowledge Creation*. Westport, CT: Quorum Books.

Bales, R. F. (1958). Task roles and social roles in problem solving groups. In E. E. Maccoby, T. M. Newcomb, and E. L. Hartley (Eds), *Readings in Social Psychology*. New York: Holt.

Bennis, W. G. and O'Toole, J. (2005, May). How business schools lost their way. *Harvard Business Review*, 96–104.

Bennis, W. G. and Shepard, H. A. (1956). A theory of group development. *Human Relations, 9*(4), 415–437.

Berger, P. L. (1967). *The Sacred Canopy: Elements of a Sociological Theory of Religion*. New York: Doubleday Anchor.

Bikson, T. K., Cohen, S. G., and Mankin, D. (1999). Information technology and high-performance teams. In E. Sundstrom (Ed.), *Supporting Work Team Effectiveness* (pp. 215–245). San Francisco: Jossey-Bass.

Bion, W. R. (1959). *Experiences in Groups and Other Papers*. New York: Basic Books.

Boukreev, A. and DeWalt, G. W. (1997). *The Climb*. New York: St Martin's Press.

Breashears, D. (1999). *High Exposure*. New York: Touchstone.

Breivik, G. (1996). Personality, sensation seeking and risk taking among Everest climbers. *International Journal of Sport Psychology, 27*, 308–320.

Bromet, J. (2005). *Makalu Gau: The Untold Story of the 1996 Everest Tragedy*. Seattle, WA: Mountain Zone. Retrieved January 18, 2006, from http://classic.mountainzone.com/climbing/misc/gau.

Brown, R. (2000). *Group Processes* (2nd ed.). Oxford: Blackwell.

Carlsson, B., Keane, P., and Martin, J. B. (1976). R & D organizations as learning systems. *Sloan Management Review, 17*(3), 1–15.

Clark, R. W. (1976). *Men, Myths and Mountains*. New York: Thomas Y. Crowell.

CNN (1996, May 13). U.S. climber, thought dead, rescued from Mount Everest. Retrieved January 18, 2006, from http://www.cnn.com/US/9605/13/everest.

Coburn, B. (1997). *Everest: Mountain Without Mercy*. Washington, DC: National Geographic Society.

Colin, N. (1996). Obituaries: Bruce Herrod: 1958–1996. *The Geographic Journal, 162*, 360–361.

Digenti, D. (2001). Lessons from Everest: The role of collaborative leadership in crisis. *The Systems Thinker, 12*, 2.

Douglas, E. (2005, November). Inside Nepal's revolution. *National Geographic*, 46–65.

Druskat, V. U. and Kayes, D. C. (1999). The antecedents of team competence: Toward a fine-grained mold of self-managing team effectiveness. In M. Neale and E. Mannix (Eds), *Research on Groups and Teams* (vol. 2). Greenwich, CT: JAI Press.

Druskat, V. U. and Kayes, D. C. (2000). Learning versus performance in short term project teams. *Small Groups Research, 31*(3), 328–353.

Druskat, V. U. and Wolff, S. B. (2001). Building the emotional intelligence of groups. *Harvard Business Review, 79*(3), 80.

Duckworth, E. (1996). *"The Having of Wonderful Ideas" and other essays on, Teaching and Learning* (2nd ed.). New York: Teachers College Press.

Eagan, S. and Stelmack, R. M. (2003). A personality profile of Mount Everest climbers. *Personality and Individual Differences, 34*, 1491–1494.

Earley, P. C., Connolly, T., and Ekegren, G. (1989). Goals, strategy development, and task performance: Some limits on the efficacy of goal-setting. *Journal of Applied Psychology, 74*(1), 24–33.

Edmondson, A. C. (1999). Psychological safety and learning behavior in work teams. *Administrative Science Quarterly, 44*(2), 350–383.

Edmondson, A. C. (2003). Speaking up in the operating room: How team leaders promote learning in interdisciplinary action teams. *Journal of Management Studies, 40*(6), 1419–1452.

Edmondson, A. C., Bohmer, R. M., and Pisano, G. P. (2001). Disrupted routines: Team learning and new technology implementation in hospitals. *Administrative Science Quarterly, 46*(4), 685–719.

Elmes, M. and Barry, D. (1999). Deliverance, denial, and the death zone: A study of narcissism and regression in the May 1996 Everest climbing disaster. *Journal of Applied Behavioral Science, 35*(2), 163–187.

Emerson, R. M. (1966). Mount Everest: A case study of communication feedback and sustained group goal-striving. *Sociometry, 29*(3), 213–227.

Freud, S. (1959). *Group Psychology and the Analysis of the Ego.* New York: Norton (first published 1922).

Gabriel, Y. (2004). *Myths, Stories and Organizations.* Oxford: Oxford University Press.

Gardner, H. (2006). The HBR List. Breakthrough Ideas for 2006. *Harvard Business Review, 84*(2), 35–63.

Ginnett, R. C. (1990). Airline cockpit crew. In J. R. Hackman (Ed.), *Groups that Work and Those that Don't* (pp. 427–448). San Francisco: Jossey-Bass.

Gruenfeld, D. H. and Hollingshead, A. B. (1993). Sociocognition in work groups: The integrative complexity of individual and group conceptualization. *Small Group Research, 24*(3), 362–382.

Hackman, J. R. (Ed.) (1990). *Groups that Work and Those that Don't.* San Francisco: Jossey-Bass.

Hackman, J. R. (2002). *Leading Teams.* Cambridge, MA: Harvard Business School Press.

Harvey, J. B. (1996). *The Abilene Paradox and Other Meditations on Management.* San Francisco: Jossey-Bass.

Helmreich, R. L. (1997). Managing human error in aviation. *Scientific American, 276*(5), 62–67.

Homans, G. C. (1950). *The Human Group.* New York: Harcourt Brace Jovanovich.

Jangbu, L. (1996). Response from Lopsang Jangbu Sherpa. Outside Online Summit Journal. Retrieved May 12, 1997, from http://outside. away.com/peaks/fischer/index.html.

Janis, I. L. (1972). *Victims of Groupthink.* Boston: Houghton Mifflin.

Kayes, D. C. (2002a). Dilemma at 29,000 feet: An exercise in ethical decision-making based on the 1996 Mt. Everest disaster. *Journal of Management Education, 26*(3), 307–321.

Kayes. D. C. (2002b). Conversational learning in organization and human resource development. In A. Baker, P. Jensen, and D. Kolb (Eds), *Conversational Learning: An Experiential Approach to Knowledge Creation.* Westport, CT: Quorum Books.

Kayes, D. C. (2003). Proximal team learning: Lessons from United Flight 93 on 9/11. *Organizational Dynamics, 32*(1), 80–92.

Kayes, D. C. (2004a). The 1996 Mt. Everest climbing disaster: The breakdown of learning in teams. *Human Relations, 57*(10), 1236–1284.

Kayes, D. C. (2004b). The limits and consequences of experience-absent reflection: Implications for learning and organizing. In M. Reynolds and R. Vince (Eds), *Organizing Reflection.* London: Ashgate Publishing.

Kayes, D. C. (2005). The destructive pursuit of idealized goals. *Organizational Dynamics, 34*(4), 391–401.

Kayes, D. C. (2006). Organizational corruption as theodicy. *Journal of Business Ethics.*

Kayes, A. B., Kayes, D. C., and Kolb, D. A. (2005). Experiential learning in teams. *Simulation and Gaming, 36*(3), 330–354.

Kegan, R. (1994). *In Over Our Heads.* Cambridge, MA: Harvard University Press.

Kennedy, M. (1996, September). By the book. *Climbing, 163,* 94–104, 147–156.

King, P. M., and Kitchener, K. S. (1994). *Developing Reflective Judgement.* San Francisco: Jossey-Bass.

Klein, G. (1999). *Sources of Power: How People Make Decisions.* Cambridge: MIT Press.

Knight, D., Durham, C., and Locke, E. (2001). The relationship of team goals, incentives and efficacy to strategic risk, tactical implementation and performance. *Academy of Management Journal, 44,* 326–338.

Kolb, D. A. (1984). *Experiential Learning: Experience as the Source of Learning and Development.* Englewood Cliffs, NJ: Prentice-Hall.

Krakauer, J. (1997a). *Into Thin Air.* New York: Villard.

Krakauer, J. (1997b, May). Everest: A year later. *Outside, 22,* 5, 57–62, 147–149.

Lawrence, P. (1987). Historical development of organizational behavior. In J. Lorsh (Ed.), *Handbook of Organizational Behavior.* Englewood Cliffs, NJ: Prentice-Hall.

Lester, J. T. (1983). Wrestling with the self on Mount Everest. *Journal of Humanistic Psychology, 23*(2), 31–41.

Lewin, K. (1948). *Resolving Social Conflicts.* New York: Harper & Row.

Maclean, N. (1992). *Young men and fire.* Chicago: The University of Chicago Press.

Marinko, Y. (1991, December). A culture of after-action review. *Air Force Magazine,* 36–41.

Maslow, A. H. (1998). *Maslow on Management.* New York: John Wiley.

Meyers, P. (1983). *K2.* New York: Dramatists Play Service.

Miller, P. (2003, May). Everest 50 years and counting. *National Geographic,* 34–37.

Mills, T. M. (1967). *The Sociology of Small Groups.* Englewood Cliffs, NJ: Prentice-Hall.

Mitchell, R. (1983). *Mountain Experience: The Psychology and Sociology of Adventure.* Chicago: University of Chicago Press.

Nelson, T. O., Dunlosky, J., White, D. M., Steinberg, J., Townes, B. D., and Anderson, D. (1990). Cognition and metacognition at extreme altitudes on Mount Everest. *Journal of Experimental Psychology, 119*(4), 367–374.

O'Dowd, C. (1999). *Just for the Love of It.* Excerpt available online; retrieved January 18, 2006, from http://www.cathyodowd.com/ev96/96_team.html.

Ortner, S. B. (1999). *Life and Death on Mt. Everest.* Princeton, NJ: Princeton University Press.

Outside Online (1997, July). *Summit Journal 1996. A Day on Mount Everest* [transcript from a benefit in memory of Scott Fischer held at the American Alpine Club, Golden Colorado]. Retrieved January 18, 2006, from http://outside.away.com/peaks/fischer/july13.html.

Padayachee, N. (2002, June 23). Everest leader flees mountain of debt. *Sunday Times*. Retrieved January 18, 2006, from http://www.suntimes.co.za/2002/06/23/news/news07.asp.

PBS Online. (2000). *Lost on Everest: The Search for Mallory and Irvine*. Retrieved January 18, 2006, from http://www.pbs.org/wgbh/nova/everest/.

Pittman, S. (1996). Sandy's Everest Journal. Retrieved April 18, 1997, from http://www.nbc.com/everest.

Popper, M. and Lipshitz, R. (1998). Organizational learning mechanisms: A structural and cultural approach to organizational learning. *Journal of Applied Behavioral Science, 34*(2), 161–180.

Rasmussen, J. (1988). Approaches to the control of the effects of human error on chemical plant safety. *Professional Safety*, 23–29.

Rasmussen, J. (1990). Human error and the problem of causality in analysis of accidents. *Philosophical Transactions of the Royal Society of London. Series B. Biological Sciences, 327*(1241), 449–460.

Roberto, A. M. (2002). Lessons from Everest: The interaction of cognitive bias, psychological safety, and system complexity. *California Management Review, 45*(1), 136–160.

Roberto, A. M. and Carioggia, G. M. (2003). *Mount Everest—1996* [Harvard Business School Case Study #9-303-061]. Cambridge, MA: Harvard Business School.

Rose, C. (Host) (1997, October 16). *Mountain Without Mercy* [broadcast transcript #2010]. New York: Rose Communications.

Rose, C. (Host) (1998, March 23). *Climbers describe expedition to Everest as "triumph"* [broadcast transcript #2122]. New York: Rose Communications.

Ross, J. and Staw, B. M. (1993). Organizational escalation and exit: Lessons from the Shoreham nuclear power plant. *Academy of Management Journal, 36*(4), 701–732.

Rostrup, M. (1998). Mount Everest: A deadly playground. *British Medical Journal, 316*(7124), 81–82.

Sashkin, M. and Sashkin, M. G. (2003). *Leadership that Matters*. San Francisco: Berrett-Koehler Publishers.

Schweitzer, M. E., Ordonez, L., and Douma, B. (2004). Goal-setting as a motivator of unethical behavior. *Academy of Management Journal, 47*(3), 422–432.

Seijts, G. H. and Latham, G. P. (2005). Learning versus performance goals: When should each be used. *Academy of Management Executive, 19*(1), 124, 127–131.

Sundstrom, E., DeMeuse, K. P., and Futrell, D. (1990). Work teams: Applications and effectiveness. *American Psychologist, 45*, 120–133.

Useem, M. (2001, October). The leadership lessons of Mt. Everest. *Harvard Business Review, 79*(9), 51–58.

Von Furer-Haimendorf, C. (1984). *The Sherpas Transformed*. New Delhi: Sterling Publishers Private Limited.

Virgil. (1982). *The Georgics*. Trans. L. P. Wilkinson. London: Penguin Classics.

Weber, M. (1964). *The Sociology of Religion*. Trans. E. Fischoff. Boston: Beacon Press.

Weick, K. E. (1993). The collapse of sensemaking in organizations: The Mann Gulch disaster. *Administrative Science Quarterly, 38*, 628–652.

Weick, K. E., Sutcliffe, K. M., and Obstfeld, D. (1999). Organizing for high reliability: Processes of collective mindfulness. *Research in Organizational Behavior, 21*, 81–123.

Weiner, E. L., Kanki, B. G., and Helmreich, R. L. (Eds) (1995). *Cockpit Resource Management*. San Diego, CA: Academic Press.

About the Author

D. Christopher Kayes is Professor of Organizational Behaviour at The George Washington University, USA. His research includes 35 papers and numerous consulting engagements around the world. He has won several awards, including best paper in 2004 in the journal *Human Relations* for *The 1996 Mt. Everest Climbing Disaster: The Breakdown of Learning in Teams.* His paper *Experiential Learning and Its Critics: Preserving the Role of Experience in Management Learning and Education* was one of three best papers for 2002–2003 in the Academy of Management Learning and Education, nominated alongside Henry Mintzberg and Jeffery Pfeiffer. He received the "New Educator" Award from the Organizational Behavior Teaching Society for promise in innovative teaching and scholarship.

He is International Visiting Research Fellow with the Centre for Management and Organizational Learning at The University of Hull. He holds an affiliation with the Sigur Center for Asian Studies and has taught in the Executive Leadership and Singapore Institute of Management Programs at George Washington. He has been affiliated with the Helsinki School of Economics and Butler University.

His website is www.theoaktongroup.com.

Index